NeXtFest Anthology

Plays from the Syncrude NeXt Generation Arts
Festival 1996-2000

SuperEd
CHRIS CRADDOCK

Benedetta Carlini
ROSEMARY ROWE

"No. Please–"
SEAN CALLAGHAN

The Key to Violet's Apartment
PAUL MATWYCHUK

Tuesdays and Sundays
DANIEL ARNOLD WITH MEDINA HAHN

EDITED BY GLENDA STIRLING

Prairie Play Series: 20/Series Editor, Diane Bessai

neWest

Canadian Cataloguing in Publication Data
Main entry under title:

A Next Fest anthology

(Prairie plays series ; 20)
Plays from the Syncrude Next Generation Arts Festival.
ISBN 1-896300-37-5

1. Canadian drama (English)—Alberta—Edmonton.* 2. Canadian drama (English)—20th century. I. Stirling, Glenda, 1973- II. Series.
PS8315.5.P73N49 2000   C812'.608   C00-91692-8
PR9198.2.P68N49 2000

Editor: Glenda Stirling
Editor for the Press: Diane Bessai with the assistance of Bradley Moss and James DeFelice
Cover design: Brenda Burgess
Cover artwork: Dale Nigel Goble
Interior photos have been produced with the kind permission of the photographers.

 Canadian   Patrimoine
Heritage   canadien

THE CANADA COUNCIL | LE CONSEIL DES ARTS
FOR THE ARTS | DU CANADA
SINCE 1957 | DEPUIS 1957

NeWest Press acknowledges the support of the Canada Council for the Arts and The Alberta Foundation for the Arts for our publishing program. We also acknowledge the financial support of the Government of Canada through the Book Publishing Industry Development Program (BPIDP) for our publishing activities. NeWest is also grateful to Syncrude Canada Ltd. for its contribution to this project.

Syncrude

Theatre Network and NeXtfest, the Syncrude NeXt Generation Arts Festival acknowledges the support of the Canada Council for the Arts, The Alberta Foundation for the Arts, Syncrude Canada Ltd., TELUS, Big Rock Breweries, the City of Edmonton and the Edmonton Arts Council.

NeWest Press
201-8540-109 Street
Edmonton, Alberta T6G 1E6
(780) 432-9427
www.newestpress.com

1 2 3 4 5 04 03 02 01 00

PRINTED AND BOUND IN CANADA

Contents

Introduction   1
BRADLEY MOSS AND GLENDA STIRLING

SuperEd   12
CHRIS CRADDOCK

Benedetta Carlini   45
ROSEMARY ROWE

"No. Please—"   76
SEAN CALLAGHAN

The Key to Violet's Apartment   110
PAUL MATWYCHUK

Tuesdays and Sundays   137
DANIEL ARNOLD WITH MEDINA HAHN

Biographies   184

Glenda Stirling introducing the new play Cabaret at NeXtFest (Photograph courtesy of David Williamson)

The Story of NeXtFest at Theatre Network

with Bradley Moss and Glenda Stirling

1. THE SEEDS ARE SOWN: BRADLEY'S PERSPECTIVE

As the original festival director and ongoing festival producer, I am honoured to have participated in the birth of the Syncrude NeXt Generation Arts Festival. This multidisciplinary festival, designed to focus on the development of emerging professional artists, was first presented by Edmonton's Theatre Network in June, 1996. An annual event since that time, NeXtFest develops the voices of the next generation of playwrights and performing and visual artists. The plays you are about to discover represent this new generation of creators.

Theatre Network has always been committed to developing and producing new plays from senior writers in Western Canada. By the mid-nineties, however, artistic director Ben Henderson was becoming concerned at the lack of support in Edmonton for the next generation of emerging playwrights. The situation was aggravated by the recent demise of the Citadel Theatre's TeenFest and the University of Alberta's suspension of its MFA playwriting program. At the 1995 Edmonton Fringe Festival, Ben Henderson approached me with the idea of starting a young writers' workshop reading festival (similar to Workshop West Theatre's Springboards).

Although I applauded the intention, I was not in favour of creating yet another public reading festival. To me the new generation needed an opportunity to showcase its finished work. Also, Henderson's original idea, in my view, was too focused on the playwright. A festival for young artists should extend its sights to the other disciplines—music, dance, film, and visual art. Theatre Network would then be fostering both the development of the young playwright and an entire generation of other artists—including those whose creativity make the production and performance of the playwright's work possible. I was more interested in creating a meeting place where young artists could exchange ideas and feed one another's creativity and hopefully establish artistic relationships early in their careers. And the event must also have a celebratory feel to it. If Theatre Network were to commit to this larger vision of support, then I would gladly accept the challenge. My expansion of the festival idea was accepted, with the condition that I raise the funds. Thus it all began. In November of 1995, I joined Theatre Network and set to work.

In that first year as the festival director and producer, I spent most of my time (when not fundraising) discovering the young artist scene in Alberta. I had graduated in the spring of 1995 from the University of Alberta with a MFA in DIRECTING. Even though I had been in Edmonton since the fall of 1992, I really had no idea of the talent that was out there. I discovered during that eventful year a richness in emerging artistic talent directly linked to the University of Alberta, Grant MacEwan Community College, the Edmonton Fringe, and the Edmonton high schools. The city has a solid tradition of training, creating, and producing professional theatre. Now as I look back, I am amazed at the number of relationships I established in the first year of the festival: Glenda Stirling (now the festival director), Deirdre Murphy (now the festival dramaturge) and the following artists to whom I was introduced in 1996, and who, some five years later, are my working peers: Chris Craddock, Kevin Kruchkywich, Rosemary Rowe, Paul Matwychuk, Sean Callaghan, Clinton Carew, Aaron Franks, Vanessa Porteous, Kathryn Bracht, Sandy Paddick, Trina Davies, Murray Utas, Sophie Lees, Sharla Matkin and many others.

In that first year, I established the play submission and selection process in place today (although I was alone in selecting the plays). The process was a little more aggressive then because none of the young artists knew anything about the festival and had to be convinced to trust us with their work. There were 25 submissions in the first year, compared with the 60 or more we receive today. The dramaturgy was started in the first year but was primarily entrusted to the directors, with help from Deirdre Murphy, Joanna Falck, Ben Henderson, and myself. We had two designers, Lori-Lynn Pedersen and Mariko Heidelk, who, with very little budget, designed all the elements for the four main-stage productions. Now we have one designer per production and supply both technical and production support, as well as professional training experience.

The festival had some great music that first year. *Captain Nemo, Kissing Ophelia, Nowhere Blossoms, Royal Family*, and *TrioHouse* rocked out on Theatre Network's Roxy stage. Phil Hawes curated and presented film from FAVA—Edmonton's Film and Video Arts Society (he continued to perform this task for the next three festivals). As well, the National Screen Institute with Anthony King's help curated an evening of film. The visual art was curated by ANOSA—A Network of Student Art Society. In addition we had two exciting high school productions (*Never Swim Alone*, from Spruce Grove Composite High School and *Seeds*, from Victoria School for the Arts), both winners from the Alberta High School Drama Festival.

When NeXtFest '96 was over, I knew we'd struck the right chord with our innovative, multidisciplinary programming. "I hope Network plans to continue this festival," our audience and participants told us. There were no free T-shirts the first year, and no free beer, yet we all knew something very special had been created. In my five years with NeXtFest, I have only found one similar event—in New Zealand—that engages a generation of artists in a multidisciplinary festival.

Without the support and guidance of the first festival advisors (read festival angels) none of this would have been possible: Dennis Baker, Gail Barrington-Moss, Diane Boudreau, James DeFelice, David Hennessey, Ben Henderson, Andy

Laskiwsky, D'Arcy Levesque, Paul Manuel, Conni Massing, Nancy Power, Kurt Spenrath and the board members of Theatre Network. The same must be said of all the artists (too many to list) who joined us and trusted us in our first year to put their new work on stage. Syncrude Canada Ltd. has been our generous title sponsor from the beginning. Rosealie Barnes and the Syncrude owners continue to believe in the dreams of the emerging artist.

2. GLENDA'S PERSPECTIVE—1996

In 1996 over 200 emerging professional artists participated in the first Syncrude NeXt Generation Arts Festival. I was one of them, proud to be receiving my first paycheque out of university. I had arrived! I could make money at this theatre thing. It was a pretty glorious feeling.

I came to NeXtFest straight out of a BA in DRAMA at the University of Alberta, essentially riding director Kathryn Bracht's coattails. Kathryn, with whom I had worked while she was completing her MFA thesis, was directing "No. Please—" by Sean Callaghan. She asked me to be stage manager—which turned out to be only one of the many roles I have since played at NeXtFest. In that rush of working on a new play, friendships and working relationships were forged. In addition to Kathryn and Sean, I worked with actors Kevin Kruchkywich (now a successful Calgary based-actor), Murray Utas (who participated in subsequent festivals) and Sharla Matkin (who went on to direct for NeXtFest in 1999 and 2000). I am proud to say that all these people have remained a part of my personal and artistic life.

What I remember most about that first festival was the excitement of working with like-minded artists on spanking new scripts. And thinking that a four-hundred-dollar production budget per show was big. (Some things never change. Each show still has the same production budget.) And beer. And a lot of laughter. We had no idea what we were doing! But somehow it all worked out, even though up to the last minute we didn't know if we'd get paid, if the set would be painted, and if anyone would come to see our shows (the posters didn't arrive until two days into the festival). But somehow it all came together. Audiences came, and we had a great time.

3. THE FESTIVAL GROWS: BRADLEY'S PERSPECTIVE—1997, 1998

For NeXtFest '97, I pushed myself to create a philosophy for the festival so I could more clearly articulate its intentions to others. I wrote out a mandate, feeling the utmost importance of focusing the festival's vision with a statement that could be used as a guideline or framework. I make it public now as the manifesto that clearly focused me, and therefore others, on what we were trying to create:

> *To provide advisement, mentorship and partnership in all matters in creating an uninhibited multidisciplinary annual summer festival. To build an association of emerging professional artists through the support, practice, and celebration of the visual, theatrical, and musical arts, thereby creating opportunities for the discovery, cultivation and dissemination of their immediate, needful, and truthful voice.*

This statement guided my efforts on our developmental support of new work, and the realization that the festival was perhaps more about developing and educating the emerging professional artist than just providing a performance opportunity. It was the first year we firmly entrenched the role of the dramaturge on each new play. It was the first year we created a festival selection committee. Deirdre Murphy, Joanna Falck, and I read all the submissions (40) and selected the plays to produce and workshop. Deirdre and Joanna continued as the festival dramaturges and we began our building blocks for the extensive dramaturgy that we have in place today (as Glenda describes below).

With NeXtFest '97, we discovered another role, which was to create a springboard for the work to a life beyond NeXtFest, for example, by providing a venue for the Stomp-style work of the dance production *RhythMatix*. Other initiatives that year included our effort to celebrate and disseminate the visual element with the Graffito Wall by Dale Nigel Goble and his "Silver Screen" painting that was our poster and T-shirt image. We also had the première of a new play, *mona*, the musical by Nicholas Little from Calgary's Alberta Theatre Projects' youth program, Theatre Blitz (where I had participated as an instructor and, through Eugene Stickland, was introduced to some of Calgary's emerging artists). Our music was stronger, with bands such as *Painting Daisies, Blue Locutus* and *Hookahman* rocking the Roxy stage. We also received generous support from community foundations, the Clifford E. Lee Foundation, The Winspear Fund, and The Edmonton Community Foundation.

NeXtFest '98 was coined "The Art of a Generation" by *Vue Weekly*. It was the festival of partnerships, growth, and the completion of initiatives that we were unable to perform in 1997. We finished the 8' x 44' Big Rock Graffito Wall, "Ballyhoo" by Dale Nigel Goble (his 1999 creations are on the cover of this book). We added a songwriters series (with Luann Kowalek, Chris Smith, Wendy McNeil, Maren Ord and Ben Spencer) that offered the more intimate environment of the Roxy Theatre lobby, and we took our bands around town to offsite venues: *Laminar Flow* and *Bell Jar Blues Band* to Sidetrack Café; *Reign* and *Blue Locutus* to New City Likwid Lounge; *A-Jo* and *rensliP* to the Windsor Bar and Grill. We expanded the number of workshop readings from six to ten and we had ACCESS Television's Speaker's Corner. (I am told our out-takes were the highlight of the ACCESS Christmas party!)

It was the biggest and most unruly festival to date with more artists, more shows, and more events than ever. And we even managed to raise the artists' honoraria. But I also discovered that the festival had become too large for one person to facilitate. We needed a festival director who could free me to work more on artist development and fundraising. I asked Glenda Stirling to fill this position because she had been involved in the first and third NeXtFests, and she had the background as actor, playwright, director, and administrator to perform well in the role of festival director. I feel blessed now that she accepted, but little did she know what was ahead of her.

4. NEXTFEST 1998,1999: GLENDA'S PERSPECTIVE

At NeXtFest '98, I had a great time directing Rosemary Rowe's *No One Showed Up for the Anarchist Rally*, and formed ongoing friendships and working relationships. In addition to Rose, I worked with stage manager Linda Knopke, designer Narda McCarroll (an MFA design candidate who has since graduated and gone on to work for Studio Theatre, Fringe Theatre Adventures, Free Will Players, and many others), and actors Heidi Taylor, Kate Connell Banigan and Araxi Arslanian. Perhaps the most important contact I made that year was dramaturge Deirdre Murphy, with whom I have since worked on six other productions, both inside and outside of NeXtFest.

I recall standing on the crowded sidewalk in front of the Roxy after a performance of *Anarchist Rally*, when Bradley Moss invited me to be the 1999 festival director. I agreed without even thinking about it, delighted to play a part in the development of this exciting training ground, showcase, and party. I like to think I would have jumped at the chance even if I had known the amount of work involved.

NEXTFEST '99:

As I headed into my first year as festival director, I faced funding cuts, desperate calls for last-minute sponsorships, and 250 artists hungry to present their work. Fortunately I was not alone. Bradley Moss was still festival producer, crunching numbers, scrounging sponsors, booking bands, and keeping me from full-out panic. Kevin Hendricks, Theatre Network's publicist, became another festival producer. Production manager Bruce Hennel and his team of technicians led the designers, directors and stage managers through the production process, leaving me free to worry about the art and administration. Festival dramaturge Deirdre Murphy was a rock of knowledge and optimism. Involved in the festival every year, she not only had a sense of the festival's history, but also a clear vision for the future. We headed into NeXtFest '99 confident that our partnership could bring the festival to another level in development and in artist and audience expectation.

Deirdre and I were committed to improving the dramaturgical component of the festival. Joined by Kyna Hamill, as a committee of three we read and, for the first time, provided dramaturgical feedback to every submission, and chose the mainstage and workshop line-ups. We also gave much thought to the role of dramaturge in the festival, especially who should dramaturge particular productions—given the strengths, weaknesses, and experience of the artists involved in each project. The expansion of the developmental aspect of the festival was key to our vision of the growth of the emerging playwright. We pushed back submission deadlines and auditions, trying to ensure that each step in the evolution of the plays—dramaturgy and rewriting, rehearsal and production—got a little more time and attention.

My partnership with Deirdre was the beginning of a new era for NeXtFest. Through our past work together, both in the festival and beyond, we had developed a strong, shared artistic vision: our commitment to developing female playwrights, directors, and dramaturges, and our sense of the festival history and vision for its future. These benefits are obvious, but also we both felt that the reading committee would continue to need an opposing view, a fresh eye and new way of looking at the festival as a whole. Kyna supplied these in 1999. The festival dramaturgical committee had always had three members (Deirdre, Bradley Moss and Joanna Falck in years previous), and Deirdre and I felt that our vision had grown so closely aligned over the past three years that we would continue to need that third and somewhat more removed eye.

By the end of NeXtFest '99, I was exhausted, elated, and a great deal wiser. We saw the festival grow: two dance shows, under the name of DanceFest at NeXtFest, were made possible through a partnership with Alberta Dance Alliance, and at the urging of dancer Amy Schindell; new sponsors and programs, such as the Telus Mentorship Program; five mainstage shows; ten workshops of new work in development, including two film scripts; a series of short works; eight visual artists; a feature-length film; eight singer/songwriters; and five bands—and a larger audience attendance than ever before. Not so bad for the little festival that could.

Dramaturgically, the festival has always had two streams, the mainstage and the New Play Cabaret. Each February, six to eight shows are selected for the mainstage by the dramaturgical committee from a general call for submissions. Mainstage selections are provided with a director, dramaturge, designer and stage manager, each hired by the festival director, and this team spends approximately four to six weeks working on the script, going through rewrites and ensuring that the text is in good shape for rehearsals. The director then casts the show, and Theatre Network provides rehearsal space, and production assistance, including technicians and crew to build the set and to run lights and sound. Each artist involved in a mainstage show gets a festival pass, a T-shirt, and an honorarium. Each production receives three performances on the Roxy stage over the course of the festival. Plays selected for the New Play Cabaret are assigned a director and dramaturge and given a public reading over the course of the festival at the Sugar Bowl Cafe on 124 Street. The New Play Cabaret is one of the best attended events in the festival, providing an opportunity for both novice and well-established playwrights to present their work for audience feedback while their plays are still in process.

5. NEXTFEST 2000: GLENDA'S PERSPECTIVE

With eight mainstage shows, eight workshops of new work still in development, and two radio plays, NeXtFest's theatre component has grown again! And dance, visual art, film and music continue to expand as audience and artist demand grows each year. This year Deirdre and I welcomed Wojtek Kozlinski as a member of the NeXtFest dramaturgical committee. As director, dramaturge and raconteur, he has proven an important addition to the team. And as the lone male voice of the selection committee, he has saved us from becoming ChickFest.

We have stepped up the dramaturgical component, allotting

approximately six weeks to dramaturgy and play development of the mainstage shows before they go into rehearsal. As well, the artistic teams have had the much more instructive and fruitful experience of weekly dramaturgy meetings with our committee to ensure that the novice dramaturges, directors, and playwrights are getting feedback and support throughout the process.

This extended commitment has been exhausting and time-consuming, but well worth it. The plays and playwrights are being developed more deeply than ever before, and the invest-ment will pay off in the rehearsal hall and down the line, as NeXtFest gets an ever-increasing reputation as a good develop-mental playground, and we see NeXtFest plays and artists take their place on professional stages.

THE FUTURE: BRADLEY'S PERSPECTIVE

Each year, as we listen to ideas from emerging artists on how to improve the festival, we see a future filled with new artistic partnerships and growth. A program of brief new works, Have You Seen My Shorts? was proposed by Matt Kowalchuk for NeXtFest '99 and has now become a regular addition to the fes-tival. We now have submissions from all across Canada, and although at present we are financially unable to bring them to Edmonton, it is our hope someday to include their voices at NeXtFest. We continue to introduce initiatives such as NeXtFest 2000's CKUA Live Theatre Broadcast, and it is only the lack of resources (read: money) that limit the potential available to us. We see a future where our festival is not only multidisciplinary but produces interdisciplinary work, combining the forums of artistic disciplines into a new style of theatrical expression—a fusion, so to speak.

The upcoming generation of artists has taught me persever-ance and the possibilities of more initiatives. I feel privileged to have helped in generating a festival focused on the immediate and truthful voice of the emerging artist that will shape Canada's artistic scene in the future. And perhaps that is what this anthol-ogy really is—a peek at the future.

I can clearly see the impact of the festival on my career and personal life. From that first and subsequent festivals, I found relationships with fellow directors, playwrights, actors, and dramaturges that will last my career. The gaggle who participated in those first few festivals has continued to work together both at NeXtFest and elsewhere, nursing each other through professional and personal triumphs and disappointments. In short, we have been developing a community of up-and-comers which now not only criss-crosses the country, but the globe.

In 2000, as we start pushing thirty rather than twenty, and begin to outgrow the festival, we, the first crop of NeXtFest graduates, still remain involved, dedicated to promoting and nurturing the festival, and mentoring new batches of artists. Deirdre Murphy has remained with NeXtFest and is taking on more responsibility each year as head dramaturge. Actor and dancer Amy Schindell, whose brainchild was DanceFest at NeXtFest, remains our dance advisor. Playwright and filmmaker Clinton Carew has remained each year to advise on developing film scripts. Actor/director/playwright Steve Pirot has moved to dramaturging new plays, and many more continue to return to explore other areas—actors returning as directors, playwrights returning to direct, dancers returning to act. And slowly, with a mixture of reluctance, pride and excitement, we are stepping aside to make room for the next of group of artists.

It has been my pleasure to work with the some 250 new and returning emerging artists and technicians who flood this theatre every June, whose passion, vision, energy, and talent fuels this festival. This anthology is the culmination of five years of support for the emerging artist, the playwright in particular. Each of these plays represents an opportunity for you, the reader, to have a look at the first steps of the artists who will be the future of Canadian theatre.

—May 31, 2000

Chris Craddock as Ed in *SuperEd*, NeXtFest 1996 (Photograph courtesy of Devin MacDonald)

SuperEd

by Chris Craddock

SuperEd is a funny and touching coming-of-age battle between the fundamentalist television religiousity inflicted upon the protagonist and the comic book idealism he has acquired for himself. Underneath the lightening character switches, the great "trouble light" acting, and hilarious jokes is a simple story of a young boy searching for a hero. A showcase for the author, or any actor who takes it on, its fast-paced multiple characterization demands precision, energy, and inventive theatricality. While this journey towards manhood is one of Craddock's best crafted tales, it is also the first of many outrageous caricatures of prairie manners and mores to follow, often combining his fascination with popular culture, and always with a keen ear for contemporary idiom.

By the time he wrote and produced *SuperEd*, Craddock already had a head start, having written, directed, and self-produced under his own company, Those Terrible Children. He began writing *SuperEd* in 1996, during his final year in the BFA ACTING program at the University of Alberta. His experience and training as an actor were important to the development of this play and to his emerging style as a writer/performer who creates lively characters with unabashed showmanship.

In preparation for an independent production of *SuperEd* in the fall of 1996, Craddock workshopped the play with Bradley Moss for the New Play Cabaret at NeXtFest '96 and by the time of this public reading, *SuperEd* was already a polished piece. For the production to follow that October, the playwright invited his classmate and later NeXtFest participant, Steve Pirot, to direct. They built the set and rehearsed the show in Chris's basement. Perhaps it was the result of working in a dark basement that Craddock hit on the inspired idea of using a simple and inexpensive trouble light as a prop and an actual lighting instrument. In production, the trouble light was more than the sum of its parts. Suspended by a simple pulley, it was used like a lasso to trap the young hero, to signify other characters, or to light small areas of the stage or the performer's body.

After the NeXtFest reading and subsequent independent production, Craddock mounted *SuperEd* again for the 1997 Winnipeg Fringe and brought it back to Edmonton to perform off-site (BYOV) during the Edmonton Fringe; simultaneously he was performing in *Indulgences*, his new play directed by friend and NeXtFester, Glenda Stirling. Craddock continued his association with NeXtFest on subsequent occasions: in 1998 for a workshopped reading of his full-length *On Being a Peon*, produced that season by Rapid Fire Theatre, and in 2000 with his one-woman piece, *Porn Star*, dramaturged and directed by Glenda Stirling and Ron Jenkins. At the 2000 festival he also contributed to the new CKUA Live Theatre Broadcast with *Luck*, an adaptation of an excerpt from a novel by Miriam Toews. Now fully professional as an actor and playwright, to date he has written or collaborated on over a dozen plays, including another highly successful and award-winning one-man show, *Ha!*, co-written with Wes Borg and performed by Craddock. Each subsequent play is different, but each has some element of the "funny-ouch!" tone found in *SuperEd*—make 'em laugh at all the things that make us cry.

—G.S.

SuperEd was first presented as a staged reading at the New Play Cabaret, NeXtFest 1996, June 19-23, performed by the playwright. In October of that year it was then produced by Those Terrible Children Theatre, Edmonton, at B Scene Studios, directed by Steven Pirot and again featuring Chris Craddock. In 1997 this production was remounted for the Winnipeg Fringe Theatre Festival, followed by an off-site run during the Edmonton Fringe Theatre Festival at B Scene Studios.

THE CHARACTERS IN ORDER OF APPEARANCE
(all are performed by the actor)

> Ed: an imaginative eighteen-year-old boy
> Lyle: Ed's cynical twenty-three-year-old brother
> Carl: Ed's evangelical step-father
> Mr. Walsh: Ed's English teacher
> Annabel's ex-husband: a hostage
> Annabel: Jimmy Swaggart's biggest fan
> Anchorman
> Cult member
> Cockney friend
> Pregnant girl
> Dumb friend
> Cat
> Homeless man

THE SETTING

The several locales in contemporary Edmonton (except for a short trip to the ultraverse) where Ed's storytelling takes him.

PRODUCTION NOTES

The stage and set directions are those of the first Edmonton production but are in no way binding to performer or director. Fast pacing of the actor's speech is essential.

SuperEd
for Derek

Darkness. There is an armchair on stage with Ed in it, reading a comic book. Hanging from the ceiling is a trouble light, which Ed uses in his storytelling throughout. The stage is littered with comic books and a basketball. Ed has hidden his Playboy *and* Soldier of Fortune *magazines under the cushion of his chair. The lights come up and he notices the audience. Ed reads to the audience from his comic book, one phrase per page, faster and faster until the end.*

Ed: Jor-el knew the planet was going to be destroyed—so they went to a show, Zorro I think it was—and he put his child in a tiny space pod—except muggers were waiting around the corner—on a small planet called Tattoine a young boy named Luke lived with his uncle—while the boy and his parents were taking a wrong turn, Gotham's full of them— the small space pod was hurtling toward earth with the boy inside—and the family walked into the alley with the muggers—and Luke met a man called Ben Kenobi who became like a father to him—and the small space pod landed on earth—meanwhile a young acrobat was training with his family—and the muggers shot the parents of the boy before his very eyes—because Luke didn't have a father of his own—and the space pod was found by a kindly old couple named the Kents who never had any children of their own—and the acrobat family was killed leaving the boy an orphan—the boy in the pod was an orphan— Young Bruce Wayne was now an orphan—now Luke had Ben Kenobi and later Yoda—and the small boy in the pod had the Kents—and Bruce Wayne approached Dick Grayson and was like a father to him—and they were like a father to him—and Mr. Kent was like a father to him—but then he died—and then Ben died—Bruce Wayne didn't die—then Yoda died—Batman didn't die—and then Darth Vader died, but you know…he had it coming. *Blackout.*

Ed takes a position centre stage. Lights up on Ed.

Ed: Okay, here's what happened. It was the day before my eighteenth birthday and I was shopping with Carl down at the Safeway, because I have to, because he needs me to carry the groceries back and I have to, because I still live under their roof, and he won't bring the car to the Safeway because, get this, HE RESENTS THE HANDICAP PARKING SPACES! He thinks that it's a big conspiracy and that only rich people get those stickers and its not a handicap thing at all. So I'm distancing myself the way I do when I'm in public with Carl. I'm great at it. You can't even tell we're together. And if he talks to me I look at him like he's crazy and I say really loud, "GEE OLD MAN I MUST JUST LOOK LIKE YOUR SON. I'M SURE NOT HIM." Safeway is really the only place he takes me to anymore because everyone knows us here and I'm not fooling anybody. Anyway, I'm standing by the comic book rack, comparing the prices with down at the store where I have my discount. And the Green Lanterns are such a rip-off, but anyway...

That's where I met him.

He came right up to me and his breath sort of smelt funny and he was wearing a trench coat, but it was long and dirty, and his trench coat slipped open and he was wearing a shirt, but it was really tight and the gut had a set of pecs on him, like woah, and his shirt had a shiny sort of emblem on it. His chin was really strong and I thought he sort of looked like a, *music: superhero sound dah de da,* but this is Edmonton and those things don't happen. And he's standing really close to me now, like I'm here and he's here and...his eyes have grabbed mine and are choking them by the cornea. *Ed swings the light and stands in the centre of its circumference.* And suddenly I'm sucked into his eyes! And I'm in the middle of this big courtroom, and surrounding me are these huge disembodied heads looking at me and all the heads are different but the same, with long wizened faces and a billion years old all over their eyes, and the middle one, the one in charge, the one that's oldest and wisest of them all, *moving forward with his arms extended, Ed causes the light to swing toward him and away behind him,* looks deep into me and reaches deep into me, and pulls out a shiny bit of something like maybe my soul.... I'm back in the Safeway, and the celery have forced a huge conga line around me, kicking their cellulose legs, the tropical fruits are leaping like spawning salmon from one box to another, rainbows are coming out of the produce sprinklers, twining around my legs and arms, blowing up my clothes and there was a voice and the voice said,

"GIVE 'EM HELL, ED."

And all the fruits and vegetables rush back to their places before the stock boys notice and I look in my hand and there's a ring. Like a get-it-out-of-a-vending-machine ring. And it's shiny like my soul. *The sound of a clear bell.*

I took it home and my brother was visiting. Despite his University studies, drug use and other hobbies, my older brother still finds time...to piss me off. He pisses me off a lot because he likes to come where I'm watching television and he likes to critique what's going on in the commercials.

Ed, as his brother Lyle, settles into the chair. The trouble light becomes the glow of the television, which is turned off and on as the channels change.

Lyle: Oh right. Like if I eat this Mr. Big, I'll grow into a freaky pituitary giant like Shaquille O'Neal and make ten million dollars a year dunking a...oh and this one. Like polar bears drink Coke. Like a father polar bear gives a shit about his cubs. They mate and they're gone and what's this computer animation shit. If you can't capture the true mating habits of a polar bear, fuck you, you know...I AM CANADIAN, like this beer is trying to tap into a referendum-based, trumped-up, crisis-style patriotism that has the depth of a puddle...Simpsons...they're cool... And Frootopia, what are they selling? Some blissed out version of a kinder gentler global fucking village via the euphoric influence of overpriced ice tea from concentrate, it just disgusts me, it just...SUCK MY COCK!

Ed: It pisses me off a lot. You don't criticize television. What else do we have, you know. I mean there's a whole little world in there, and it's not like our world, I know that. But you can look at it and figure out stuff. You got to get an example from somewhere? You got to get heroes from somewhere, right? I've been thinking a lot, and I read some books and I asked my brother some stuff, and I think it sort of breaks down like this. Okay, in the old days, like okay, really, really old days, you have kings and queens. They're the heroes. And it's the old days, right, so you don't have television, so you don't really know what's going on. *Ed makes his way to the chair where he transforms into Lyle.*

Lyle: The queen is probably fucking the archbishop and the king summers in Devon with eight young squires. *Stands as Ed.*

Ed: But nobody knows, because they're in the palace and we're not and they have a power, a light, a mythic something that comes from on high and they are the heroes. Then, like lots, lots, lots, lots, lots later, you have sports stars, astronauts, war heroes. They can do what you can't. They can score a billion goals, *music: da le da da DAAAH! as Ed mimes a hockey triumph,* and travel to space, *funky space music as Ed floats weightless,* and kill German people, *sound: explosions,* and you can't, so they're the heroes. And we know a little more. Joe DiMaggio is married to Marilyn Monroe, but they're not so happy. Jackie Kennedy is a babe but her husband still screws around, maybe with Marilyn Monroe. There's information in the air, but its foggy. Now— *Ed transforms to Lyle.*

Lyle: —all the baseball players are coked-up billionaires, the Apollo moon landings were probably faked, at least I think so, and the Prince of Wales is quoted having voiced a desire to be someone else's tampon.

Ed: It's a big hero drought. So people look around for new heroes and they can be found in two places, on TV and in comic books. TV heroes are good, they drive expensive cars, they have excellent musical backup, they're faced with clear moral choices and usually can be counted on to do the right thing, except, *as if telling a secret,* they're actors. They are. And they're actors with money, because they get to be on TV shows, so pretty soon they're not on the good TV show being a hero, they're on the bad TV shows and people are talking about their overdoses and their bulimia and their divorces and their overdoses and when you see the hero next, he's tainted. He's different. He's dirty. Who wants to look up to a divorced drug-addicted bulimic? I can get that at school. Comic book heroes are better. They don't do anything you don't see them do. They are always themselves, and who they are…is good. It's simple.

My mother, however, is complicated, because God is living in our guest room. His real name is Carl, but he acts like he's God. They started out sort of boyfriend-girlfriend, but now they're different. Carl sleeps in the guest room and

Mom looks away when he talks to her, like he was too shiny to look at. And sometimes he says things, stupid things, and Mom will embroider them and hang them around the house. Like "Dance if you love Jesus" over the fridge and "I only hate what God does" on the piano. Years ago, when I was a kid, I remember playing with my Superman doll and flying it around and saying, "Mom, Superman can do anything!" and she said, "oh no honey. Only God can do anything." And then Carl knocked on our door.

Ed as Carl grabs the trouble light and holds it like a briefcase, using its glare to punctuate his holier thoughts.

Carl: Hi there, my name is Carl Tribinski. I am with the Church for the Punitive and Celebrational God. Dear lady, do not shut your door. I am here with an important message that could save you and your family from the fires of hell where demons would feast on your entrails forever. You are not a judgmental person. I can tell by the way you hold your eyes, level, not looking down on anything. I know you don't want your neighbors to be damned to hell, and wouldn't it be nice to be responsible for the salvation of your entire block? It would, wouldn't it, and what's more, God, *turns on the light to illuminate his face,* will thank you for it too. *Carl is invited in.* Now I can tell by your eyes, and as I stand closer, by your perfume, that you don't care what people do in their own homes. It's a hard world and whatever makes people happy is okay with you. What you worry about is salvation. *Holds the glowing light up in his hand to be admired.* Because these people think that God comes with a lot of rules and they won't be happy following him and they might tempt, *notices a younger Ed and talks to him,* your children with that attitude and then when you take your first class trip to heaven, where will your children be? *In childish tone to Ed*: Where will you be? In the gaping maw of Satan, writhing in the acidic saliva of the Dark Lord himself. Yes you will! Yes you—*Ed is frightened away.* I feel what frightens people away from God is the rituals that religion has chosen to surround him with. I mean who wants to eat the flesh of Jesus, pretty darn distasteful, and I can see, *shines the light in Mom's face, with seductive aside,* from the delicate curve of your breast that, *back to normal,* you think so too. And who wants to ask Jesus into their heart?

There's a lot of undigested red meat in there for him to trip on and I can tell, *light in Mom's face,* by the quiver of your beautiful buttock, *back to normal,* that you agree. So how can we entice the faithless? By making the trip to heaven a joyous one and by sealing the path to salvation in a light-hearted manner. *Holds the light up to his chest, covering it with a hand.* With this sung prayer I can save the souls of any who wish it, heathen or angel alike. I would like to show it to you and I can tell, *light, seductive tone,* by your baited breath and taut puckered nipples, *normal,* that you'd like to see. Join me in this and go to heaven.

Carl puts the light up to his face where it becomes a sort of glowing mask as the music turns from holy to eerie. Blackout.

Ed: And he's been here ever since. *Lights up on Ed.*

My real dad died a long time ago. I was eight. He died in a very strange way. You see, now this is complicated. We were in the backyard, in the shed, he was fixing something, he had one of those drill-screwdriver-gun things, he was screwing something to the wall or something and he was standing in my turtle pool and there was a little bit of water in the bottom. He slipped on the water and dropped the drill into the puddle he was standing in, which gave him a shock. But that didn't kill him. The shock sort of sent him off balance and he fell onto a rake handle, broken rake handle, broken like jagged and it poked into his stomach. Pretty far. But that didn't kill him. I was helping get to the house, and my brother was practicing to get his learner's permit, so he was practicing backing in and out of the driveway, in and out of the driveway, in and out of our driveway, and he hit dad with the car. But that didn't kill him. We got him into the house and we sat him down and we called an ambulance. And he was hurting pretty bad so Mom got him a Tylenol, and it was one of those Tylenols those crazy people put the cyanide in—do you remember those? And that's how he died. In a way it was good, because everyone in the family felt equally guilty. It was my turtle pool, my older brother hit him with the car, Mom gave him the Tylenol. We were all equally at fault, so in a way, we were all equally absolved. Except maybe for— *as if Ed heard her on the stairs,* Mom? Mo-om?

Anyway. Before he died and all. It was a beautiful day. He was a man, MY DAD, and I was helping him do a manly thing, fixing something. And he was happy, and singing the Air Supply songs he used to sing, and I had my Fisher Price tool belt on. It was a beautiful day. *Ed grabs the basketball.*

With our father dead and all, my brother suffered from a certain amount of paternal performance anxiety. And later, he went to university, so he felt he knew a lot about stuff. When I was still a kid he left me to Mom, then one day he walked into my room, I was thirteen and he should have knocked, it was a rule to knock, and he caught me, uh, well, he caught me. *Ed dribbles the ball, faster and faster, changing in style until he tranforms into Lyle.*

Lyle: I know what you were doing. And I'm here to tell you that I used to do it too, in fact I still do it from time to time. In fact, if I were to grow up and marry a squad of nymphomaniacal cheerleaders, I would probably still do it from time to time. So go hard, chief, whack it till you're blue, spit in your hand, get a tube of Brylcream, get blisters if it comes to that but don't feel all guilty about it, alright? Alright. Now if you're slapping skin, and you obviously are, you've probably started spouting hair in funny places and—don't show me your armpits, I can imagine, alright. Now, this is called puberty and it sucks. But it is a necessary step in the long, painful transition between boyhood and manhood. If you're popping woodies, you're on the right track, you'll need those later. Because excellent sexual performance is the first thing about being a guy. Also, driving. You gotta learn to drive as soon as you can, because if you can't drive, you can't get chicks, and getting chicks is the first thing about being a guy, also, when you're driving, and you're going somewhere, really going somewhere far away, like, I don't know, the West End or somewhere, you're there, you're in control, the radio's high, the asphalt's black and you are free, and being free, that's the first thing about being a guy. *Lyle transforms back into Ed.*

Ed: I'm eighteen now, so I'm the right age to be a guy, but I only just learned to drive, I'm a virgin, and I don't feel free. I don't even know the first thing. But I will.

Because I've got this. *Shows the shiny ring.*

I've been researching superheroes. A lot of them started out young: Robin, Superboy, The Changeling…me…and I figure that's a good way to go because the expectations are lower. Also superheroes have really good bodies, so I've been working out in the basement and my arms are getting bigger. If you look at the comics, Superboy's arms aren't nearly as big as Superman's, so it's okay to build up to it. Also, superheroes don't tend to have fathers: Superman, Batman, *indicates self*. Check! One weakness that I've been trying to deal with is a lack of solid fighting technique. I mean if you don't have amazing powers, you gotta know some kung fu or something or you're gonna get your ass kicked. A scary costume only puts them off guard for awhile, and if you don't start busting heads, they're gonna laugh at you. My brother tried to teach me how to fight, because he said holding your own in a fight is the first thing about being a guy, but even though I tried to put his concepts into action jab, jab, jab, knockout, jab, jab, jab, knockout, *sound of clapping on impact with Ed's shadowboxing,* I usually end up lying on my back kicking out with my legs. Like this. *Ed lies, kicks down and out with his legs.* People laugh, but it makes it really hard to beat your head in.

As much as I hate Carl, he's been really good for my physique. Because of his active way of praying. He believes in a joyful method of salvation, and is trying to propagate his prayer as an all-purpose, multi-denominational entrance to heaven. We have to do it every night before supper. It goes like this:

Ed does an incredibly chipper dance to the song:

My God goes, downtown baby, downtown the roller coaster,
Sweet, sweet Jesus, sweet sweet, don't let me go
Don't wanna go to hell, to the mouth of Satan
Don't wanna go to hell, to the mouth of Satan
Don't try to tempt me, won't let you
I'm going to heaven, why don't you
Salvation's like a sundae with chocolate on the top
Oooh Jesus, dig him, dig him good, they nailed him to wood
He'll cleanse me, befriend me, Satan is my enemy
He'll save me, won't enslave me
Punch Satan in the stomach with my faith

I don't think the Catholics are gonna go for it.

The other problem that superheroes have is income. It doesn't pay anything. And that's how it should be. I mean if it paid something there'd be a bunch of assholes doing it, like with the cops. Short term I can live with Mom, but I gotta get outa here sometime. It's okay, though. I have a plan. This might be hard to believe, because I don't put on airs or nothing, but I'm really smart. Like really, really smart. Like a genius. I took the test and they told me and everything.

You know how people are always saying they have that one teacher in school who meant a lot to them, changed their life and all that? I tried really hard to have one too. But I felt a little awkward with the gym teacher after failing tee-ball and the science teacher tried to kiss me. Huh. Me and the English teacher, Mr. Walsh, we got on okay for awhile, but after the test…. *Ed transforms into Mr Walsh.*

Mr. Walsh: Melancholy is a physical sensation. It's physical because it's spiritual, you see. It's as if your soul climbs out of your chest and sits on your head. It presses your brows into your eyes, makes it hard to see. It's physical insofar as they're connected. The body, mind, the spirit. The soul climbs out, leaves an emptiness, which here in North America is taken to be hunger and is the reason we are all so fat. But it's not food that is missing, though it is nourishment, nourishment. It's easy to feel like there's no point in doing anything in the world today. Ecological disaster pends at any moment, governments slaughtering their own people, the war between the sexes showing no signs of abating, and Quebec seems to be getting ready to take their ball and go home, leaving our country easy prey to the massive Americans and their terrifying machine. But aren't all these problems just a better reason to get into the fight and help out. It's like with garbage men. They don't eliminate garbage, it's always there. But the garbage men stop it from piling up, from being the only thing we see. Nobody can eliminate the problems of the world, but you can be a garbage man for the world, stop the problems from being all that people see.

Now, you're special, you've been told that, so I'm going to tell you something that I don't tell all my students. Stupid people don't matter as much. They are there to furnish the destiny of the smarter people. Everyone thinks so, no one says so, but it's true and I'll give you an example. I went to a 7-Eleven today for some cigarettes. The boy behind the counter got them for me. Now I don't know that boy, but I guessed from the blank look in his eye that he does not have my comprehensive world view, or your raw intelligence. Therefore, the entire purpose of his day was to furnish me with the nicotine I need, to keep my head clear to give you the advice you need. His destiny furnished mine, to help me furnish yours. Don't make him meaningless. Don't make him meaningless. Part of being a man, a true man, is accepting your destiny. I quote, "When I was a child, I spoke as a child, and ate as a child, and made poo-poos in my pants like a child, but when I was a man I put away childish things, and damn well wiped my own butt." I'm paraphrasing of course. And I do so to remind you that nothing is set, nothing is sacred, the great sentence goes on, and you, you may add a subjective clause. What will come before your period, Ed?

Ed: I decided not to go to university.

I invent things. The things I invent don't make me a lot of money, because I invent things that are for a specialized group. Like superheroes. I mean, not that many people need a doormat that you can electrify, or buglike tracking equipment. Its not a general market thing. My brother says if you really want to make a lot of money inventing, you should invent something for cars that makes them burn fuel more efficiently. Apparently the oil companies buy that sucker right up. It never gets made. But they'll pay a lot of money to see it doesn't. I'm still working on that. In the meantime superheroes need stuff, and if you want stuff, you need money, and the best part of being eighteen is that you get to cash your own bonds.

Me and my father spent my eighteenth birthday together. I know he's dead, but we did anyway. We went out for breakfast, just me and him. I ordered steak and eggs, rare, and had a shot of Bailey's in my coffee. We talked about Mom, and Carl and the World Cup. Mostly I talked, real quiet, so he could hear me.

And he said it was okay to cash my bond to buy unlicensed weaponry to fight crime on a volunteer basis.

With the cash from the bond, I got a short wave radio so I could listen to the police band, and a remote so I can listen while I walk around—on patrol. I bought a used Ford Escort, black, to be my superhero car, and I bought a blind guy cane and a couple of cattle prods to tape to each end. It makes a wicked electro staff and it folds up. You have to be careful to turn the prods off before you put it in your pocket. I sent away for some night vision goggles in the back of a *Soldier of Fortune* magazine and—

Have you seen that magazine? *Fetches it from the chair.* There's an article in it on how to convert the legal semi-automatic to an illegal fully-automatic and there's a form in the back to order the semi-auto. You can get a whole automatic gun with just this one magazine. *Sound: machine gun.* Huh. *Throws magazine over his shoulder.*

I didn't feel confident enough about the fighting to make a lot of arrests, but I thought I could begin some patrolling. I started with an afternoon patrol, just sort of walking around downtown, just walking and I notice someone lying on the ground on a piece of cardboard, face down. Now, I don't know first aid or nothing and I really should learn. But for this guy, I thought I better call 911. So I call. *Ed grabs the trouble light putting it to his ear.* Hold? I can't hold. I—Holding. *The light goes out to indicate the operator is no longer on the line. A long pause.*

Yes, hello. There's a guy. A guy by the Mac's. The Mac's on 97th and 102nd.

Well, I don't know, just a guy. I think he might need some help.

Who am I...I'm...*deep voice.* My name is—*Ed hangs up.*

It's important my secret identity be maintained. I decided to watch from across the street. An ambulance showed up. They got out and looked at the guy, who sort of woke up and rolled over. They were laughing, like the guy wasn't in much trouble or wasn't worth much if he was. Then a cop car showed up. Then another ambulance. Then a firetruck, then another firetruck. And they're laughing. The cops are laughing, the firemen are laughing, though a couple of them look a little disappointed that he's not on fire. And its now occurring to me that this isn't an emergency at all. Just a grown man who can't afford a place to live. Huh.

And this guy has probably never seen so much official attention in his life. The cops hang around the longest, trying to get the guy on his feet. Trying to get him on his way, 'cause you can't just sleep in front of the Mac's. People might see you there and not want to buy stuff, so he had to go. I decided to go too. It's funny how all those people showed up. There's a lot of help around. It doesn't always…help. I followed him around the corner to see if he was okay, and he was gone. Disappeared. All that was left was a trench coat. Long, dirty and familiar.

When I got home, me and Carl had a talk about my soul.

Ed holds the glowing trouble light above his head with his back to audience, as if it were Carl's glowing face.

Carl: I know you are not saved, my son.

Ed: I'm not your son.

Carl: I know that you are not the fruit of my loins, but I live here under this roof and I've come to think of you in a paternal manner, if I may.

Ed: It's your brain. Think what you want.

Carl: Now, I just want to explain to you how your mother feels about your lack of salvation.

Ed: What do you mean, Carl? I do the prayer dance thing at supper with you guys every night.

Carl: That is not a cure-all. The prayer only works if you hold it in you all the day, and try to live by the beauty it represents.

Ed: Salvation's like a sundae with chocolate on the top?

Carl: The point is, my son, that your mother worries that she'll be in heaven, looking under every rock for you, and you'll be nowhere to be found, and she will have to spend all eternity with the knowledge that the light of her mother-hood adorns the nipple ring of Satan.

Ed: Satan has a nipple ring?

Carl: Undoubtedly, for no perversion comes to the world before it has been danced out in the nightclubs of the dark Lord Beelzebub.

Ed: I didn't know that Satan did product testing. *Ed turns out the light and faces the audience.*

But Carl touches on a point. Parents who are religious, who like really believe it, must really worry about their kids who aren't. I mean worry that they'll have to hang around in heaven, forever knowing your kid just ain't coming. Huh.

Ed collapses to his knees in a scream.

AAAAAAAAAAAAAAARRRRRRRRRGGGGGGGGHHH-HHHHH!!!!!!!!!

That's the sound of my mother's friend Annabel, finding out about Jimmy Swaggart and those hookers.

Want to hear it again?

AAAAAAAAAAAAAAARRRRRRRRRGGGGGGGGHHH-HHHHH!!!!!!!!!

My mom's friend Annabel had a special penchant for Jimmy Swaggart. She had five life-sized cardboard cut-outs of Jimmy, which she would place in different spots around her house. There was one relaxing in the easy chair in the living room. One folded up at the table in the breakfast nook. One sitting on the upstairs toilet, reading a copy of *Soul Saver Weekly*, one on a stepladder fixing a light bulb, and one in the bedroom, that we weren't allowed to look at. Huh. And they all had a little tape recorder, taped to their backs, and would say little things to Annabel from tapes she'd make herself from his TV show. The words were all out of context so it would sort of sound like "Good – Morning – my – love." And stuff like that. When Jimmy fell from grace, Annabel figured it had something to do with her ex-husband. You see, her husband was always a jealous guy, so Annabel figured he was trying to come between her and Jimmy by means of this slanderous campaign. That was why she took him hostage.

But when her ex-husband was still her husband, he was a pretty cool guy. And she was a neat mom. They were a principled hipster couple, drove a Volkswagen van and were shrouded in a loving coolness that linked them with silver bonds of shiny affection that latticed the backyard, where me and my mom and dad would come over for barbecues. Him tending the tofu-kebabs and her tossing a huge salad in a wooden bowl, carved from a massive tree stump from the Claquot region. They glowed with fallout from a Sixties war of anti-nuclear hip. They were great. And while I was busy becoming an adolescent, something had changed and now they weren't.

So her ex-husband came over to pick up their son Ricky. He was on the standard-every-second-weekend-divorced-father schtick. Annabel hauled him into the house and taped him to a kitchen chair. Across from him all the Jimmies were folded up, and those Jimmies put him on trial for his life. All of them asking him questions in that weird tape-spliced stutter of his. No one knew what had happened to him, until a videotape showed up at the local TV station. It sort of went like this:

Ed grabs the light and sits in the chair, the light shining up into his face.

Annabel: *Voice off.* Read it! Read it!

Ex-Husband: "I'm here to clear the name of Jimmy Swaggart." Annabel, this is—

Annabel: *Off.* Just read it.

Ex-Husband: "Mr. Swaggart has been cruelly misrepresented, and pressured into confession by network executives, the godless heathens. He was never with any prostitutes." Annabel—

Annabel: *Off.* Read it!

Ex-Husband: "The man with the prostitutes was me, posing as Mr. Swaggart, to, to end his loving relationship with my ex-wife." Annabel, you have gone completely mad you know th—

The trouble light is snapped off. The lights come up on Ed.

Ed: And that was it. The news show had gotten the tape anonymously. They ran a phone number along the bottom to call if you had any information, but it went by too fast, so I called 911.

Ed grabs the light to use as the phone.

Ed: Hold, I can't . . .

I decided to suit up and go in.

Ed suits up in front of the light in silhouette.

Make no mistake. There is something very sexy about wearing superhero stuff. I never would have thought of it, I mean, Superman never looked particularly turned on, especially with that sort of flat way they draw his crotch, but it is heady stuff, let me tell you. Tights hugging up along your thighs, a thick heavy belt. The mask, oh man, especially the mask, hiding you, making you everyone and no one. Making you a dark hero and an animal at the same time.

Ed turns around and poses in his suit. He looks ridiculous.

It was a good thing it's a bit of a drive to Annabel's 'cause I, I needed to calm down a bit. I got to her place and she was standing in her flower beds, all alone, like an overweight sunflower. She said—

Ed pulls his cape over his head like a blanket Annabel has wrapped herself in.

Annabel: Eddie? What are you wearing, Eddie? Trying to be a hero, Eddie? Why not. Why not. It's so funny, you know. You believe in God. You really believe in him. You put all your mind into just feeling that he's there that so he is. He's in the room with you, sipping coffee. He holds your hand when you're sad, and makes you feel like there's magic and majesty and the world isn't just Wall Street and plastic and sewers and…all that. Except. Except God's a man. You always think of him that way. He did this, He did that, always capitalized, not he but He and why not—I mean He is God. But since he's a man, you just, can't quite trust him. You can't quite feel like he knows you, 'cause I'm a woman and God. God, is such a…MAN. It's not like he wasn't far away in the first place. So you build a bridge. You find a way to make the God smaller, so you can…get your mind around him and so you find a person who…sort of reminds you of God. And then there's the bigness of it all, wrapped up in a guy in a suit, a human, just like you are a human, but more. 'cause he's holding it. He's got the magic and the majesty all wrapped up in the powder blue vest of his suit and it's coming through at you with his lame Southern drawl and it's his job to make the world magic for us, and HE DROPPED THE FUCKING BALL! God, you know. He blames everything on the women and a bunch of men nail him to a cross and two thousand years later and it's still the woman's fault, but he keeps sending us these men and…where's my soul? Where's my soul?

Annabel transforms back to Ed.

Ed: I went into the house and the exhausted ex-husband was buried in shredded Jimmy. His little head poking out of Jimmy's arms and legs and all the tape recorders are going: "Good - morning - my - love - time - for - coffee - my - love - time - for - coffee - my - love - time - for - coffee - my - love - time - for - love - love - love - love".… And a little fire had been started in the pile. So it's good I got there. It could have been broiled former spouse all over the place.

Just as I was leaving, some reporters showed up. I guess my older brother had seen the thing on the news and called the campus paper, who called the cops who called the real papers. They got some pictures of me running to my car.

Ed takes a running pose while the trouble light blinks on and off three times, like flashbulbs.

The caption said "Who is this man?" I even made the TV news.

Ed runs to the chair and uses the cushion as his news desk.

Anchorman: It seems a domestic dispute was broken up on the north side of Edmonton today by no less than a masked crusader. Has Edmonton found its first superhero? Vigilantism is of course illegal, and is judged by many to be also moronic and the product of a skewed world vision, prompted most likely by unrealistic television shows and comic books that make it seem like a private citizen can improve his community without the help of government employees. Is this a crazy person on Edmonton's streets? Probably. Stay tuned, we'll be going over to the ITV lab, where one of OJ Simpson's tears is being examined for…remorse. *Anchorman transforms back to Ed.*

Ed: I don't watch that channel anymore. Annabel has a son named Ricky. And when Annabel had to go away, Ricky's dad got custody. He needs to get a bigger place and stuff so Ricky stayed at our place for a week. That meant a ton of Carl exposure. I caught Carl telling him a story.

Ed pulls down the trouble light and Carl walks around it with Ricky.

Carl: There was once a good Christian couple I knew, back in Tennessee. They had, unfortunately, misspent their youth listening to rock and roll music popular at the time, with its fornicative four-four time and blasphemous backbeat. When they accepted Christ, they put all those records away in a trunk. And that trunk somehow found its way into their infant child's room. Now the baby was crying, crying, always crying in the night, and the parents couldn't understand why, until they found that trunk of records and disposed of it properly. You see—you see there were demons in the records, whispering to the baby, always whispering to the baby in the night and thus making it cry. And the same thing could happen to you, if you don't stop listening to this…Raffi.

The lights come up on Ed.

Ed: I had to get him out of there. But, I mean, what do you do with a kid when you've got him. I mean, he's alive, right? And he doesn't know anything, but he sort of knows everything too. And you have to be careful what you tell and show him, 'cause he might forget what he knows and learn the same weird stuff that you did, but you can't just leave him to learn from his friends 'cause their parents might not have the same hands-off approach. Parenting, you know, it can drive you crazy. All it is is forty years of waiting to see if you made a mistake. I tried to remember stuff my brother had told me. I remember when I was sixteen he said—

Ed makes his way to the chair where he is transformed into Lyle.

Lyle: Being a man? Well, being a man sucks. You are born into a system of oppression. The older you get, the more you can judge your level of success as a man by your level of effective oppression. And the satisfaction level of the oppressed. Nelson Mandela said that oppression dehumanizes the oppressor as well as the oppressed. That's what being a man is. A slow process of dehumanization. Of himself, of everyone around. Look at war. Who dies? Young men. And everybody else. Who sends them to die? Old men. You just can not trust the fuckers and what's more, you're gonna be one. Sure, you try to say, I'll be different. I'll be a different kind of man than I've been exposed to so far, but you know what? You can't. It's like when you wear a suit. You walk a little different, you sit a little different, you hold yourself in a wrinkle-free way and it changes how you feel while you have it on. Well, when you're wearing all that old flesh it starts to affect how you see things. Words like RESPONSIBILITY come into play. I have a responsibility to make enough money to support my family. I have a responsibility to keep my nation's interests protected. I have a responsibility to send men to die, to burn the Wiccan midwives, to stop listening to my wife until she starts sleeping in the microwave oven, to hide behind a newspaper in the den and be the bogeyman that mothers conjure—"wait till your father comes home." I tell you what, Ed, you want to be a good man? Don't be a man at all.

Lyle transforms back into Ed.

Ed: But I can't tell a six-year-old that. I couldn't think of anything to say to, you know, mold him, so we played street hockey for a while. After that I still couldn't think of anything to say to make him well-adjusted, so we rented that Batman cartoon, Mask of the Phantazam, watched that— it's pretty good—and I still couldn't think of anything to say. So we went for ice cream and read comic books until after dinner and played in the sprinkler in the backyard after that. I still couldn't think of anything to make him feel good, but he looked pretty happy when he went to bed. Maybe I'll think of something later. I hope so. I want to be a good parental figure.

In the meantime the superhero thing wasn't going at all

well. I decided what I needed was some guidance. And for guidance, I needed the man in the long dirty trench coat. So I looked, I looked along Boyle Street. I popped into little restaurants that served beans with their bacon-and-egg specials and sell cigarettes by the each. I looked in the weird bathhouse on Jasper and 98th with the art deco sign. I bought 28 copies of the same issue of *Spare Change*.

Ed approaches a homeless man.

Ed: Excuse me, I'm looking for a guy, about six feet four, 230 pounds, really built, shiny emblem on his chest, has a way of sucking people through his eyes to another dimension where they're impressed into a knighthood of superservice?

No? Okay thanks anyways.

Ed turns back to the audience.

But nobody knew who he was. I couldn't find him. So I went home. BIG MISTAKE. I walk in the door. *Sound: slap.*

Carl: Degenerate! *sound: slap.* The Spawn of Satan be gone from this boy! *sound: slap.*

Ed: What the fuck are you doing? *Sound: slap.*

Blackout. The trouble light comes on held by Ed, who is lying across the arms of the chair.

Ed: And the lights go out and when they come on, I'm tied to the kitchen table, except we're not in the kitchen. The table's been dragged down to the basement. Surrounding me are the weirdos from Carl's prayer meetings, and Mom's there and she's crying. And Carl's got my uniform and he's stuffing it in the gas barbecue and pouring lighter fluid all over it. And I hear this weird chanting and it sounds sort of like Latin, but then I realize it's just Carl's stupid prayer song.

Cult Member: *With the light under his chin, in a low chant.* Salvation's like a sundae with chocolate on the top.

Ed: And Carl finally says,

Carl: *In full Carl form, using the light as a mask.* We have found in this boy's lodgings, under a holy roof, the gear of sin and degradation.

Cult Member: Ooooh, Jesus, dig him, dig him good.

Carl: We have found the tight black pants of homosexuality and the hockey gear of masochism.

Cult Member: They nailed him to wood. He'll save me. Won't enslave me.

Carl: Cleanse him Lord. CLEANSE HIM!

Cult Member: Punch Satan in the stomach with my faith!

Ed: And then the X-men burst in. Storm controlled the crowd, pushing them with a blast of wind against the wall, where they sort of twitched uselessly. Ice Man encases my mom in a frozen pillar, her tears in a freeze frame on her face. Wolverine gets to Carl and splits him from stem to stern with a swipe of his adamantium claws, catching his guts in a frying pan and serving them to Carl with a nice hot mustard. And with his last breath, and between bites, Carl croaks out,

Carl: I was wrong, I was wrong, Satan doesn't wear a nipple ring. *Dies.*

Ed: Except that didn't happen.

What did happen is they chanted like that for a long time. And my mother cried and I cried, 'cause these guys are fucking crazy. I thought they were going to sacrifice me or something and they finally untied me and I packed my stuff and went to my brother's pad.

When I got to my brother's place, he was painting the fridge, a huge avenging angel swooping down on the unsuspecting Egyptians. I said, "Hey, cool fridge." And he said,

Lyle: Yeah, fucking God, eh? Leads a few thousand Jews out of Egypt, parts a sea, sends the angel of death, goes to all that fucking trouble and then leaves six million on their own in World War II.

Ed: Real cheery guy.

And his roommate is rolling a joint the size of a Kryptonite bike lock and there are two girls in the living room playing Twister. One of them's pregnant. And she's winning. I rely on my knowledge of general dwelling architecture to tell me it's the living room, because there's nothing in there but a stereo, three dozen pillows and a motorcycle from the late Seventies. I turn back to my brother and he says,

Lyle: So Carl finally went to the zoo, huh? Well, *mi casa, su casa* until you figure out your gig. It's especially easy right now, being reading week. Actually suicide prevention week. Apparently around this time of year several of our future leaders of business and engineering and agriculture decide to pull a lemming act off of the campus higher buildings. So a week of semi-vacation was put in to ease off the pressure.

Ed: My brother seemed to be taking full advantage.

Lyle takes a long, long, long pull off a joint—even longer—and offers to Ed.

Ed: Moral dilemma. Superheroes don't do drugs, they fight drugs. They go to dark dens where crack mothers sell their children to swarthy faceless men in exchange for throat-searing oblivion. Drugs are the opiate of the masses, the killers of our children, just say NOOOOOOOOOOOOOOO! But on the other hand—

Lyle starts laughing, giggling.

Lyle: You're a real strange little guy. But…I love you. You know and I— *Ed reaches for the joint.* No, no, no. Uh, uh. That's not what I meant by that. You can just hang, talk to folks, it's no biggie. Are you sure? 'cause I…Okay… *hands Ed the joint.*

Ed: After all, it's reading week. I took a few tooks or tokes or whatever, and wandered into the living room. And there was something in there I hadn't seen at home in years. Conversation.

Cockney Friend: I think there should be no cars. Wait, no, I do. I think that between the cities fast trains should be set up, right, and in the cities all the roads should be taken out and a system of medium speed, huge carved swans should run on little tracks, stopping at corners. You get in, you say hi to whoever's in there. You sip your coffee and head to the office in this beautiful, environmentally friendly way. Then the world wouldn't be so uptight, right. You're late for work? Hey man, I had trouble getting a swan, no sweat, happens to me all the time. And everybody has the same swan, right, so nobody's comin' to the office showing off their new BMW swan or their Mercedes fucking Benz swan or their Range Rover swans. Transportation won't be the money moniker it is now.

Ed grabs the basketball and shoves it under his shirt.

Pregnant Girl: What if everyone in the world was born a Siamese twin? Joined at the chest and stomach, and somehow it wasn't your sister you're attached to, but your perfect life partner, your perfect boy or girlfriend, the one. And you didn't have to find them or anything. You were just born together and you're attached so it's easy to make love. In fact you could do it while in line at the bank and if you were cool about it, no one would ever know. And when you get pregnant, you both get pregnant. You both feel this new life growing inside you and you both get really hungry and you both get sick in the morning. And when the nine months are up, you both go into labour and you both give birth and you both cry and hold the baby to your collective chest and you both love it with that feral animal love that a mother has. *Dismissively.* And a father. And the child you have is a son and a daughter, or a son and a son, or a daughter and a daughter, and a perfect couple all in one, and there is no missing piece to find, or not find, in the outside world. You're born complete. What if?

Lyle: *Responding to Cockney Friend.* Sure man, that's all nice and good, but who's running the swans? The government, that's who and the trains and the planes and all the rest. Pretty soon, you can't go anywhere except where the government says you can. And what's that gonna do to the human spirit. The right to get in a vehicle and travel, by your own mind, through your own volition and end up nobody knows where but you. That's self evident to a free society.

Dumb Friend: No, that's not what I said. No, you are putting words into my mouth and I—No you got that—That's not what—Hey what are you trying—*He pouts.*

Cockney Friend: That's so 1955, man. The world is in the state it's in because there is nowhere left to go, right. We've been everywhere, right, and we've left our footprints behind so destructively that the world won't see the next century before California is the next Atlantis. What we need to do is not hop in cars and go out, but hop in our souls and go in. The human spirit is the undiscovered country.

Dumb Friend: Okay, okay, I think that gay people are just fine. Awright? And that the sexes should be equal. Awright? And that racism is bad. Awright?

Lyle: The human spirit? The human spirit? The human spirit has become a commodity so thoroughly traded it's lost all value. In the dawn of Christianity it was the watch word of the feudal system, tricking generations of serfs to slave themselves to death in hopes of a better life in the hereafter. Then the Catholic church sells, like popcorn at the movies, Indulgences to get people already dead out of purgatory, enough relics of the cross to build a set of condominiums and enough shrouds of Turin to sew together a blimp. And now it's the Nineties. *The Road Less Traveled* leads to the *Celestine Prophesy* to tell you about *The Life You were Born to Lead.* Discover your soul if you want, but be sure you wrote the road map and didn't buy it for $29.95 including a home meditation cassette.

Ed: *Nervous.* I got this ace joke. There's this horse. The horse is a racehorse and while he won some races in his youth, but he's getting old and he's way past it, and he's losing all the time. So the owner comes and he says, "Listen, there's a big race coming up. If you win, you get to retire in one of those fancy animal country clubs, if you lose, it's the glue factory." So the horse trains. He trains and trains and trains and trains. His life's on the line, so he's working super hard. The day of the race comes. He lines up with all the other horses. The gates open and he's running as hard as he can, but the horses are passing him and pretty soon he's last place. And there he is running away, thinking about becoming adhesive and he hears this voice and the voice says, "Don't give up. You can do it." And he gets inspired and he runs faster, faster than he ever thought possible, faster perhaps, than any horse has ever run before. And he wins the race. The crowd goes wild, beautiful mares neigh his name in the stables, each begging to be the first when he's put out to stud. And he gets to retire in the snazzy animal-retirement club. All the biggies are there. Benji, Hammy Hamster. And he gets talking to a group of horses. A few Kentucky Derby winners, the Black Stallion and Trigger—not a great conversationalist—and he's talking about the race. And he says, "You know, I just about lost, but this voice came to me. Inspired me, and I won." And this dog comes up and says, "What's this about a voice?" and the horse looks down and says, "Holy shit, a talking dog."

Nobody laughs.

Huh. It's a funny story, see. It has a punch line, but it's not that funny and the strangest part about it is that it goes on so long and means so little. Sort of like...life?

Ed receives approval and a joint. He takes a few tokes.

I wandered out on the porch to look around.

Ed sits in the chair.

And I looked at the moon and it was so big. When I was a kid I used to think that the moon was following me. It seemed to move as I moved and I mentioned this to the cat who I was sharing the porch with and the cat said,

Ed uses the knot of his cape as a cat puppet.

Cat: Ah, that's bullshit, man. The moon don't follow nobody around. It does what it wants and fuck you too, know what I'm saying. There's a lot to be learned from that big, round motherfucker.

Ed: Is that what you do, too?

Cat: Pretty much. I like the boys in there all right though. They'll be spared when all the shit goes down.

Ed: What shit is that?

Cat: We cats are an alien race. We were dropped off here by accident after we built the Sphinx. The mothership's coming back some day and then we are gonna kick ass and take names. Your bro and his pals though. They gonna be alright.

Ed: Then I showed him my ring.

Cat: What the hell is that?

Ed: I'm not sure, but I think it's my soul.

Cat: What are you gonna do with it?

Ed: Good things. Really good things.

Cat: Shit man. It's good enough to do okay things. You can't do too much good without doing some bad. Maybe you should stick that back inside you where it belongs and let it help you just live. Just live, man, and wait for that mothership. That's what I can do.

Ed: That's not good enough. No, see. I'm a boy, you see, and I need to be a man.

Cat: Hah. You fucking humans are all alike, man.

Ed: What do you mean?

Cat: Looking all over for a good reason to be alive. Like you gotta be a hero to make up for all that air you're breathin'.

Ed: You tell me then. What is the point? What should I do?

Cat: Well, me? I like to chase stuff. Keep clean. Eat. Take shits. Take naps. Have long comfy screws with grey, short hair kitties in heat.

Ed: Well, I can't do that.

Cat: Nope. You'll just have to figure out what you can do. And do that.

Ed: And just then I saw the man, the guy from the store. I couldn't believe it, I mean, after all that searching, here he was. He could tell me what to do and I was in a perfect state to understand, my consciousness having been freshly raised and all. I ran out to him and flung my arm around him in a huge hug.

Homeless Man: Get the fuck off! Jesus damn Christ, I wasn't even near your house, not bothering anything or nothing.

Ed: I'm sorry. I'm sorry, oh jeez, ha. It's dark, so you might not remember me. But. It's me. Me. The one you picked.

Homeless Man: The one I picked for what?

Ed: The one. From the Safeway. You picked me out, you gave me, you gave me this ring. See, the ring. You gave me this ring and you took me to this other dimension, and—

Homeless Man: Are you high?

Ed: Uh. Yeah. Yeah I am, but—

Homeless Man: You got any left?

Ed: No. No, not really. Listen, I've been trying really hard to do what I think you meant by what you did. What you wanted me to do, as I inferred by your actions.

Homeless Man: Did I tell you to do something?

Ed: No, not really, well, YEAH, yeah you said, "Give 'em hell, Ed."

Homeless Man: Pretty general advice, isn't it?

Ed: Yeah. I suppose it is. Could you. Could you tell me. Could you tell me what you meant?

Homeless Man: I had a son once. Couldn't think of a thing to tell him. I tried, I thought for years, couldn't think of a damn thing. So, when he was twelve, I looked at him, and I said, "Give 'em hell, Tony." And I gave him my watch. And I left.

Ed: You left your son?

Homeless Man: It was all I could think of to tell him. It still is, except maybe, "try to stay off the booze." So when I see a young guy with that confused look, I give him something and I say, "Give 'em hell." 'cause, that's all I could ever think of.

Ed: I see. So. You left your son with give 'em hell, and you go around and say to people give 'em hell, and that's all you mean by it and that's all you have to give me.

Homeless Man: It's all I could think of.

Ed: It's all you could think of. I did...all that I did, 'cause I thought it was my mission, that you, that you had something real for me. That you had wisdom for me. That you could give me the way to go, to get on, to be a man and you tell me, you tell me, that, it's...

Homeless Man: It's all I could think of. In the end, all anybody has to tell anybody is what he could think up. And that's all I could think up. I'm sorry.

Ed: And I watched him wander away. And he was so frail. Like a pile of raked leaves. And those pecs I thought he had, I just imagined. Just put in there to make him, to make him more than he is. Make him more familiar. And I could see him grow smaller, and the city seemed to engulf him, absorb him, eat him. He was so hard to…to stay mad at.

I was heading back to the porch and my brother was on it. He was pretty stoned. And we sat on the porch together and he turned to me with that "this is important" look on his face and he says:

Lyle: I was reading, about guys, about young guys like us and how they're having trouble being men, becoming men, and it's about the older guys. They meet the older guys and they don't like them. They don't like them at all and they think, "Oh fuck, is that what it is to be a man?" So they avoid manhood, they avoid it for as long as they can and then they get to be forty and they look at themselves and they think, "Oh fuck, I'm a man, this is what I was afraid of," and they start to not like themselves.

Ed: …and I look at the cat, and the cat seems to be smiling at me, nodding at me.

Lyle: So I figure. I figure the trick of it is to get a little chat. A little talk to guide them through, so I thought about it, a lot about it…and Dad was just a guy. He died, 'cause that's what guys do sometimes and being angry is natural, but what you got to know is that he didn't do it to piss you off, or 'cause you were a bad son or any of that. Now I know you know that, sure, but you gotta know it, inside like, or it's useless to you, for you…

Ed: …and the moon in its sky describing its circles, daring me to do the same.

Lyle: Uh. Oh, okay…okay, another thing is you can't do any one thing or any bunch of things that is gonna make you a man. I mean, you can't get your driver's license and say I'm a man. You can't boff a bunch of chicks and say bing, I'm a man. You can't join the army or get a tattoo or leave home, well you can, I mean, of course you can, but what I'm saying is that none of these things or all of these things are not gonna make you a man.

Ed: …and my ring has left a green stain on my finger, left a mark.

Lyle: Being a man. Being a man, is just…. It's just, *long pause*, well, I don't know, but it's not that stuff. Okay, the last thing, the biggest thing…is that it's good to be a man. And it's not good for all those bad reasons like getting paid more and not having to menstruate. It's good, 'cause there's warmth in there. There's strength in there. There's kindness and tenderness in there and you can nurture, you can and you gotta know that, like, really know that, inside like. And if you do. If you really do. Then you won't act like an asshole like guys do all the time. So…uh, that's it. That's it. That's the talk.

Ed: And I said thanks. And we sat there on the porch. And I thought about what he said. It was okay. It was okay, 'cause…his heart's in the right place. And it was all he could think of.

BLACKOUT

Benedetta Carlini

by Rosemary Rowe

Since high school, Rosemary Rowe has been experimenting with plays that combine quirky surface absurdity with deeper levels of introspection. *Benedetta Carlini* is the first of three works to be produced on NeXtFest's main stage over the years. The play's NeXtFest production in 1996 marked the beginning of its evolution from a one-woman show into a drama of six characters, one that deftly absorbs two contrary worlds: a 17th century Italian convent and a contemporary North American college dorm.

In the quirky present time, two modern young women, the pensive Clare and the turbulent Gwen, are engaged in rival Women's Studies projects. Clare is absorbed in her vindication of Benedetta Carlini, a lesbian nun and religious visionary of tarnished reputation—but who, like female mystics before her, was a threat to the hierarchical ordering of Catholic belief (at a period already under threat by the Reformation). Gwen, the jealous skeptic, is fixated on her own "post-feminist deconstruction" of the Anglo-Saxon epic *Beowulf* into "Beowulfa, the Need for Mead." Lesbian in inclination herself, Gwen serves in part as a comic foil to the groping visionary yearnings of Clare, a lapsed Catholic once-removed whose meagre spiritual resources include a newly acquired rummage-sale collection of religious kitsch.

On a deeper note, Rowe writes, "I set out to explore questions of faith, mysticism, sexuality and acceptance. The play's central image, for me, is the Holy Trinity vs. The Trinity of Self, which, for my purposes is one's spiritual identity, rational/intellectual identity, and one's physical/sexual identity. Idealistic Clare sees Benedetta as the embodiment of this Trinity of Self, although she herself has only the most tenuous grasp on two of the three elements." Fascinating in its examination of divine and metaphorical trinities, the play is also very funny in its explorations of interpretative dance, women's studies, and the therapeutic benefits of "glow-in-the-dark Catholic iconography."

Benedetta Carlini offers an excellent example of the role

NeXtFest plays in the development of a new work. In the pre-NeXtFest script, Clare was the speaker and also assumed the roles of the other characters. The NeXtFest version, although using five actors (with one doubling), was still in monologue form and the playwright was uncertain how well this would work in full production. However, she notes, "Hearing different voices and interaction between characters opened the door to a host of possibilities." This production, with its dancewear costumes and choral singing, also inspired the interpretive dance that introduces the play. Rowe took up the play again for her BFA thesis project, developing new possibilities of character and character interaction in *Benedetta Carlini*, this time using six actors. In the play's most recent production, she continued the process by creating a number of new scenes between the various characters within their respective time frames.

Her subsequent NeXtFest plays, *Beaten with Pastry Under Cover of Darkness: A Tourist's Tale*, directed by Trina Davies in 1997, and *No One Showed Up for the Anarchist Rally*, directed by Glenda Stirling in 1998, have yet to receive further dramaturgical attention from the playwright. The former, like *Benedetta Carlini*, hovers between two periods of time. The setting is Paris, both now and in the pre-war period. Canadian student travellers are billeted in a former insane asylum harbouring unexpected relics of a once incarcerated disciple of Antonin Artaud and his Theatre of Cruelty. The students find themselves walking a fine line between reality and fantasy, sanity and craziness that echoes the world and theatre of Artaud.

The later play is another examination of life among female roommates, a highly charged attempt to examine their daily interaction on an "internal level." This is to say, the playwright imagines what the "real world" would look like if the women expressed what they were actually feeling—about themselves and each other—in the course of their daily domestic lives together.

—G.S.

Benedetta Carlini (with the subtitle *Lesbian Nun of Renaissance Italy!!!*) was first performed in 1996 as a one-woman show at York University's playGround festival starring Julia Gray.

For NeXtFest of 1996, June 19-23, it was developed into a play for five women and produced on the main stage as follows:

Benedetta: *Kathryn Osterberg*
Bartolomea: *Audrey Armstrong*
Clare: *Claire Frances Muir*
Gwen/Investigator: *Michelle Martinuk*
Professor: *Audrey Armstrong*

Director: *Sandy Paddick*
Set: *Mariko Heidelk*
Costumes/Lighting: *Lori-Lynn Pedersen*
Stage Manager: *Trish Agrell-Smith*

Benedetta Carlini was further developed and remounted in 1997 as the playwright's thesis project for her BFA in DIRECTING at York University.

The play was professionally produced in its present version by A Rose and Two Pansies Theatre at Nightwood Studio, Toronto in May, 1998 with the following:

Benedetta: *Julia Gray*
Clare: *Joanne Boland*
Bartolomea: *Suzanne Ranson*
Gwen: *Renee Olbert*
Professor: *Liz Pounsett*
Investigator: *Christopher Kevill*

Directors: *Charles Pavia and Rosemary Rowe*
Set Design: *Drew Nelson*
Costume Design: *Jay Junnila*
Lighting Design: *David Hein*
Sound Design: *Jeff Muhsoldt*
Choreography: *Samantha Booker*
Stage Manager: *Marisa King*

THE CHARACTERS

Benedetta Carlini: a religious visionary?
Bartolomea Crivelli: a 17-year-old novice, Benedetta's
nurse and "companion"
Investigator (Stefan Cecchi): a clergyman
Clare: a 21-year-old university student
Gwen: Clare's best friend
Professor (Lilian): a professor of Women's Studies

THE SETTING

The play shifts in time and setting between 17th century Italy
and a present-day Canadian city. Scenes set in the 17th century
occur in Benedetta's convent cell and in the office of the
Investigator. Scenes set in the present take place in Clare's university dorm, the Professor's lecture hall and office, and in a
campus coffee shop.

PRODUCTION NOTES

The almost complete lack of stage directions in this play is delib-
erate. The scenes are meant to cross-fade from one to another as
seamlessly as possible so as not to disrupt the rhythm. The stage
is divided into three areas: a bedroom area, which is Clare's
room and the nuns' cell; an interrogation area, where the
Investigator works and where the Professor meets with her students; and the lectern area, where the Professor delivers her lec-
tures and the Investigator issues his reports. There are also a lot
of curtains.

The interpretive dance at the beginning is funny, but the comedy lies in the fact that they're doing an interpretive dance. The
dance itself is well-choreographed, sharp and ritualistic. In the
last two productions, the dance has been set to "Erghen Diado"
by *Le mystère des voix Bulgares*, the Bulgarian Women's Choir.

This play is based on a true story.

Michelle Martinuk as Gwen in *Benedetta Carlini*, NeXtFest 1998 (Photograph courtesy of Ian Jackson)

Benedetta Carlini

Professor: So how does it start?

Clare: *After careful contemplation.* I think it starts with an interpretive dance.

Pause.

Gwen: Tell me you're kidding.

Interpretive dance in which the entire cast, with varying degrees of clumsiness, participates.

Clare: I imagine sometimes what it would have been like to be her. Sneaking into Bartolomea's bedchamber at night, sliding under the sheets with her, whispering the most glorious words religious ecstasy could spew forth, tongues touching, long hair tossing, spread out over the pillow. A cool breeze passing over the thin gleam of sweat on their bodies, moving together in a ritual that lasts the night, Bartolomea's breath catching in her throat as her lover finds the hard knob of flesh with her hand, reaching inside, so tender and loving and husky voiced as she speaks the words of an angel and lays on hands, the sweetest corruption, the most gentle hellfire Bartolomea has ever known.

I'll tell you a secret. In the morning when I get up, I move like some heavy animal through water until that first swallow of caffeine slams into my veins and I go through my day thinking that I am awake. But at night, in my dreams, I reach out with my mind and with my body, straining to touch, slamming into cold concrete, splitting the skin of my fingertips, bleeding black.

Bartolomea sleeps as Benedetta kneels beside the cot to pray.

Benedetta: You're in my soul. You'll always remain. When You touch me, I can barely breathe.

When I first came to this place, Your Mother was waiting for me. She stood in stone by the entrance and as I knelt before Her, I told Her that I had left my carnal mother, and humbly asked Her protection and guidance. I felt Her fingers on my face, soft as rose petals blown by wind, soft as dust, but when I looked up, She was cold and hard, a statue with arms outstretched. I knew then that Her eyes were on me.

My body felt like stone. Cold and hard, a statue with arms outstretched, but when You brushed aside the curtain between our worlds, filling my body with Your angels, the stone turned to silk, a flood of light in my blood. I am grateful, Lord, for Your gifts. I am full of joy.

She's in my soul. She'll always remain. When We touch her, I can barely breathe.

Professor: Let's talk about lesbianism in the Middle Ages, mmmmmm? I assume we've all done the reading, yes? Some of us? Ooookay. We assume, of course that lesbianism was being practised during the Middle Ages, but the few documented cases of homosexual sex between women, i.e. women who got CAUGHT, took place, for the most part, in monastic communities. Yes, that's right, whoever whispered "The nuns were fucking." At this time, however, lesbianism was pretty much on the same level as masturbation, both being mortal sins, and not much was done about it, barring, of course, the separation of the two sisters in question. Basically the Church had no clear guidelines for lesbianism because they simply could not imagine what two women could DO with each other without that greatest of all organs, the penis. Ah, now THAT got your attention, didn't it, Carlo? Well, young man, there's no reason to be embarrassed—I tend to be somewhat startled myself when the word "penis" pops up in a lecture. Pardon the pun. Heh, heh.

Investigator: "Papers relating to the trial of Benedetta Carlini, abbess of the Theatine nuns in Pescia, who pretended to be a mystic but was discovered to be a woman of ill repute."

Gwen: So get this. I'm helping Mary Ellen shave her head in the bathroom and that fuckin' Nadia walks by with that guitar she can't play and says, "Hey, Gwen! If you need any, like, guitar for your new project, you guys let me know, 'kay?" and I think, "If I see you with that guitar one more time, I'm going to BEAT you with it" and then I think, "WHAT new project?" and so I say, "WHAT new project?" and she goes, "Well, I was just chatting with Clare and she was telling me this weird story about this lesbian nun and how she wants to write a MUSCIAL about it and so I was thinking…" and her mouth kept on moving, but I stopped hearing because I was thinking, "Lesbian NUN Musical. HMMMMMM. THAT doesn't sound much like our post-feminist deconstruction of *Beowulf*."

Clare: Gwen, you missed the BEST lecture this afternoon.

Gwen: I did the reading, Clare.

Clare: Well, don't you think it's an amazing story?

Gwen: What's this? What's in here?

Clare: Oh, just some stuff I picked up downtown…

Gwen: This is JESUS.

Clare: Well, it's a candle, Gwen. It just happens to have Jesus ON it.

Gwen: And this is a keychain that just happens to have the Holy Virgin on it.

Clare: Yeah…

Gwen: Rosary beads. Holy water. Clare?

Clare: Yes?

Gwen: This glows in the dark, doesn't it?

Clare: Yes, Gwen, it does.

Pause.

Gwen: What the yellow, rubbery fuck are you doing?

Clare: I don't expect you to understand, okay, I'm not sure that I get it myself but this stuff, it makes me feel…closer.

Gwen: Closer to what?

Clare: Well, to her. To Benedetta.

Gwen: To WHO?

Clare: Benedetta Carlini! Lesbian nun of Renaissance Italy! I thought you said you'd done the reading!

Gwen: I DID do the reading, you whore! I just hadn't expected her name to sound so DUMB out loud.

Clare: Aw, fuck you, Gwen.

Gwen: Yeah? Well, fuck you TWICE.

Gwen exits. Clare starts after her, thinks better of it and starts to decorate.

Clare: *Trying it out.* "Benedetta Carlini. Lesbian Nun of Renaissance Italy."

Professor: Where was I? Oh yes—Benedetta. The story of her life and her rise from a poor country girl to abbess of a city convent is ferociously interesting; her very speedy and somewhat unexplained fall from that position is even more so. It was widely believed that Benedetta was blessed from birth, hence her name, which means? Anyone? Bueller? Yes, that's right, Max. It means blessed. So gratifying to know that those walkman earphones are just in for show. Benedetta entered the order of the Theatines at the tender age of nine. At the age of twenty-three, Benedetta came to the mother superior of the convent to tell her that she had been having visions of Christ and the Virgin Mary. Knowing that Satan often had a hand in these sorts of things, the mother superior told Benedetta that she should pray to Jesus to replace these tricky visions with "travails" (illness or physical suffering that indicated the Almighty's desire to test her). Her prayers for travails were answered; she began to experience such intense pains over her entire body, especially at night, that she was often paralysed by them. "Travails" is a French word. Can anyone tell me what the translation is? Fran? Could you tell us? It means "work," Fran. Look into it, all right?

Bartolomea: Sister Benedetta?

Benedetta: *She has an Exedrin headache.* Who's there?

Bartolomea: Forgive me, Sister, for interrupting you at prayer...

Benedetta: There is no fear of that, Sister. The whole of my life is a prayer.

Bartolomea: Oh, of course. Forgive me for...for...I...

Benedetta: I make you nervous.

Bartolomea: No, Sister, I...

Benedetta: Why?

Bartolomea: Sister?

Benedetta: What have you to fear from me? A true bride of Christ fears nothing…with the possible exception of Sister Carmelita's meat stew.

Bartolomea: *Smiling.* I'm sorry, Sister. You are not as I…as I was told to expect.

Benedetta: Because I'm not bleeding or speaking in tongues?

Bartolomea: Well…

Benedetta: You must understand, Sister, that my body and behaviour, when not touched by God, are those of an ordinary woman, like yourself.

Bartolomea: We hear your cries clear on the other side of the abbey, Sister. Mother Superior tells us of your visions, your trances and your travails. We pray for you and for Jesus to deliver his message to us through you. Forgive me, Sister, but it seems to me that you are anything but ordinary.

Benedetta: What is your name?

Bartolomea: I am Bartolomea.

Benedetta: You are a postulant here?

Bartolomea: Yes, Sister, for nearly three months now.

Benedetta: And how is it that you have been chosen for this position so early in your postulancy?

Bartolomea: My father is a physician here in Pescia. During the plague, I helped him to nurse the sick…the Mother Superior knew of my experience and no one else was as suited…

Benedetta: Or willing…

Bartolomea: Yes, or willing to undertake the task as I. Mother Superior says…

Benedetta: Yes?

Bartolomea: She says…

Bartolomea reaches out and places her hand on Benedetta's forehead.

Bartolomea: That I have a healing touch.

Pause.

Benedetta: It seems you also have a gift from God.

Bartolomea: He has brought me here to ease your pain.

Benedetta: The pain is how I know He's here.

Bartolomea: Of course.

Benedetta: So. It is nearly dusk. I take what little food I can here in my cell. If the trance is to come, it will begin during the evening prayer. You will come to me after your supper in the dining hall?

Bartolomea: Yes, Sister.

Benedetta: Then you may go.

Bartolomea: Thank you, Sister.

Benedetta: Oh, and Bartolomea…do not be afraid. I hear they're serving fish tonight.

Bartolomea: Unfortunately, Sister Carmelita has a unique way with fish as well.

Benedetta: I will pray for you.

Bartolomea smiles, crosses herself and leaves.

Investigator: "As recorded by Monsignor Stefan Cecchi on the 12th of October in the year of our Lord 1626:

Sister Benedetta Carlini, reputed mystic and nun of the Theatine abbey in Pescia, came to my attention in the year of our Lord 1619, soon after she claimed to have been married to Christ in a somewhat elaborate four-hour ceremony that was witnessed by the congregation on the 27th of May, the day of the Holy Trinity. The claims made by Benedetta Carlini with regards to her mystical experiences needed to be evaluated to determine two things. Firstly, that her assertions could be verified by witnesses and secondly, that her visions of God, her alleged exchange of hearts with Christ and the appearances of wounds of Christ upon her body were not a result of demonic possession. So soon after the great plague and, *he shudders,* the

Reformation, we can certainly not afford to have any of our potential candidates for sainthood proven fraudulent by anyone but ourselves."

Gwen: Jesus Christ!

Gwen points out all the Jesus-related objects in Clare's room.

Gwen: Jesus, Jesus, Jesus, Jesus, Jesus, Julie Andrews, Jesus, Jesus, Jesus, Mary, and Joseph! What the crumbly buffalo fuck is going ON here?

Clare: There was a sale at the Daughters of St Paul! The nuns helped me pick it all out!

Gwen: Okay, okay, look…I am not for a second suggesting that you stifle your, uh, creative impulses here, okay, but NUNS? NUNS?! You're not even CATHOLIC. Where is this obsession COMING from?

Clare: It's not an obsession, it's…an avid interest…

Gwen: Look around you, Clare! One lesbian nun story and a week later you've got a room full of votive candles and a rosary as BIG AS YOUR BODY. You have JESUS FOR A NIGHT LIGHT and I don't even want to KNOW where you got the "Areala: Warrior Nun" action figure from…

Clare: Gift.

Gwen: Clare, you are talking about women who are married to the big J.C., okay? They pray. They dress. They pray. They eat. They pray. They grow BEARDS for God's sake! They pray. They sleep. They try to solve a problem like Maria. They pray. They wear those goth outfits…you know? Okay. I'm not denying the potential for comedy there, but NUN-SENSE, baby! It's been DONE.

Clare: Benedetta Carlini is NOT NUNSENSE.

Gwen: Oh I dunno about that Clare, that Rue McClanahan always looked a bit butch to me.

Clare: If you don't shut up, I'm going to feed you this candle.

Gwen: Alright, alright, I'm sorry. But think about it, Clare. Who gives a wet slap about some ole lesbian nun in Renaissance Italy who almost managed to pass herself off as a saint but turned out to be a BIG LIAR? She was a FAKE. She was a FRAUD. WHO CARES?

Clare: I do.

Gwen: You do.

Clare: Yes.

Pause.

Gwen: Fine. Fine. You go ahead and write your "Bernadette Corleone" dyke nun megamusical. When you're ready to return to "Beowulfa—The Need for Mead," you just let me know.

Clare: Gwen.

Investigator: Your name?

Clare: *Quietly but firmly.* It's "Benedetta Carlini."

Bartolomea: Bartolomea Crivelli.

Gwen: EAT me, Clare.

Exit Gwen.

Investigator: Your age?

Bartolomea: Seventeen.

Investigator: And you are the candidate's nurse?

Bartolomea: *Confused.* I don't...

Investigator: Sister Benedetta, you are her nurse.

Bartolomea: Yes, Monsignor.

Investigator: And how long have you held this post?

Bartolomea: For the past six months, Monsignor.

Investigator: And you share her cell.

Bartolomea: Yes, for at night she needs me almost constantly. She is in such pain, Monsignor, that it would break your heart.

Investigator: The pain is the sign of God's love, Sister Bartolomea.

Bartolomea: Yes sir.

Investigator: You are aware that we are investigating Sister Benedetta…

Bartolomea: Because she might be a saint.

Investigator: Did she tell you that?

Bartolomea: No, Sir, your scribe did. Outside. In the hall. Just now.

Investigator: I think it's time for that boy to take a vow of silence.

Bartolomea: Sister Benedetta feels humbled and unworthy of the Lord's gifts, Sir. She never claims to be anything more than one of the Lord's many earthly vessels.

Investigator: Tell me, Sister—in the time that you have served Sister Benedetta, have you witnessed anything that might lead you to believe that she has been directly in contact with God?

Bartolomea: Yes, Sir.

Investigator: Well?

Bartolomea: Yes, Sir?

Investigator: Can you describe it?

Bartolomea: I am frightened, Monsignor.

Investigator: You have nothing to fear from me. Begin at the beginning.

Bartolomea: *Closing her eyes, in the moment.* I was with her every night as the knives in her body tried her over and over, doubling over in pain, curled up tight, weeping, weeping. I would do what I could to comfort her, wiping the cold sweat from her face, whispering prayers, stroking her hair.

She told me to return to my cot in a voice soft as snow falling. I left her side, but watched as she lay back on her bed…

Peeking out from behind the curtain, seeing—I am frightened, sore afraid, yet pulled towards her. She reaches out, eyes open but unseeing, locked in love with Him, her chest rising up, splitting open, a light

I cannot

Cannot see her

I blink

She is back on her bed, tears running silent down her cheeks, trembling

She turns her head and sees me

Trembling

She beckons with her eyes

"Here," she whispers, screaming. "Here. He's in here"

And I reach out and touch her chest. Her heart. And my hand…my hand is on fire

As the moment ends, Bartolomea starts, as if from a dream, to find Benedetta in her cell.

Benedetta: Bartolomea…

Bartolomea: Sister…forgive me, I did not hear you calling…

Benedetta: Peace. You need your rest.

Bartolomea: Is there something you need?

Benedetta: You work from dawn until sundown and then from sundown until dawn.

Bartolomea: It is a privilege.

Benedetta: I wonder sometimes where you find the strength.

Bartolomea: In you, Sister.

Benedetta: In the trance, through the pain sometimes I hear His voice. He tells me that He loves me and that I must not be afraid. Sometimes, in the darkness, I confuse His voice, His touch, with yours.

Bartolomea: I want only to comfort you.

Benedetta: On the nights when the nightmare is at its worst, He sends an angel to help me bear the pain. The angel fills me with love and with joy and the pain grows distant. He is with me now. He is inside.

Bartolomea: *Kneeling.* I humble myself before Him.

Benedetta: He has seen your compassion and your tenderness. We have come to thank you.

Bartolomea: Your hands are shaking.

Benedetta: You are so beautiful.

Benedetta takes Bartolomea's hand and draws her to her feet. They kiss.

Benedetta: I love you. You must not be afraid.

They kiss again as the lights fade.

Gwen: Picture it—BEOWULFA. All she wanted was a cup of mead and all of a sudden, there she is: alone in the great hall, the stone floor wet and sticky with the blood of dead warriors, awaiting the arrival of her foe, the lone fighting woman in a standoff with the dragon Grendel...

Professor: The ultimate symbol of the dominant patriarchy!

Gwen: I get CHILLS just thinking about it!

Professor: GOD, I love post-secondary education!

Gwen: But, no. Clare decides to take time off from the project to work on the show-stopping dyke nun megamusical number, "MY HAND IS ON FIRE." I guess I shouldn't have yelled at her. It is kind of an interesting story, and sure NUNSENSE has been done, but, let's face it— NUNSENSE was crap.

Professor: Indeed. Benedetta's saga offers far more in terms of plot, the rise and fall of a great or not so great woman in history. Regardless of the veracity of her claims, she did accomplish...

Gwen: *Cutting her off.* Personally, I think Benedetta's big mistake was pulling a Jesus. I mean, she was a powerful woman, feared, respected, you know, I mean, NOBODY fucked with Bennie, aside from Bartolomea, of course, but pulling a stunt like that? Trying to emulate the Resurrection? I mean, that's, like, INVITING the Pope to crawl up your ass with a microscope. She could have gotten away with it all, the visions, the stigmata, exchanging hearts with the big J.C., even the wedding ceremony, she could have been a saint, for Christ's sake, but she WENT TOO FAR. She screwed up and when the investigator showed up a second time, she ran out of friends REAL fast. That's the part of the story that Clare just can't accept, you know, that Benedetta fabricated the entire thing. She wants to believe that Benedetta was persecuted by jealous nuns and back-stabbing priests. I personally think Clare's full of shit on that count but I'd never tell her that because...well...

Professor: Because you love her, and you don't want to hurt her because you know that she is the kind of woman who will hate you forever if you continue mocking what matters to her.

Pause.

Professor: My undergrad was in psych.

Clare: There are no drawings, no images of her, but in my head, I see her clearly. She had piercing eyes and long slim hands and her belief in God was so so strong that she bled from her palms, her forehead and her feet. I don't know how to describe this...connection, really...

Professor: Mmmmm?

Clare: It's like...Through four hundred years of dust, pale ink and official Church documents, I have uncovered a living, breathing woman. Her image hangs just behind my eyelids; I feel sometimes that I can reach out and touch her, as if the years between our lives can be brushed away like cobwebs. I want to speak with her, but can't begin to find the words. I want to tell her that she has something I'm missing, something I need.

I...I don't...or can't or won't believe in God...I was raised by a couple of ex-Catholics...

Professor: Ah. All of the guilt and none of the absolution.

Clare: But I still have a tremendous respect for those who believe in THEIR god. In their church. I guess that I'm a great believer in belief. And the amount of faith one would have to have in order to dedicate one's life to the service of a being that may or may not exist is inconceivable to me. What does that much faith look like?

Investigator: Tell me what you see.

Professor: I think it must be beautiful.

Benedetta: A small girl leads me up a treacherous path. I slip many times along the way and she takes my hand as I am about to fall. She surprises me with her strength. She tells me that the strength is mine.

Investigator: Then what do you see?

Benedetta: We are in a garden. Jesus is there and His Mother, Mary. They welcome me and tell me not to be afraid. They tell me that each time They call me to them, the path becomes more treacherous. They tell me that soon my faith alone will help me over the stones.

Investigator: What do they look like? Can you actually see them?

Benedetta: No.

Investigator: Then how do you know that you are truly seeing the Son of God?

Benedetta: Their glory blinds me.

Investigator: Has it not occurred to you, Sister Benedetta, that Satan may well choose these glorious shapes with which to tempt you? That your weakness as a woman makes you prey to his tricks?

Benedetta: He sits across from me and asks me questions. I see him through a haze of pain. Today there is no one in my body but me. I am careful to give the right answers, for no one else is here to speak for me.

Investigator: When did the travails begin?

Benedetta: Have I been abandoned?

Investigator: In this nightmare, can you see who it is who causes you this pain? Is it the Evil One?

Benedetta: I struggle to draw aside the curtain, invite the angel, but the fabric has turned to stone.

Investigator: And the wounds of the stigmata appeared before or after the "wedding to Christ"?

Benedetta: He examines my palms, my forehead, my feet. The blood is dry. He looks suspicious. Without the wounds, I have no proof.

Am I lost?

I know only what I have seen. What I have felt. What I feel.

Investigator: Since your wounds are not much to look at, perhaps you could describe the experience.

Benedetta: It begins with my forehead. Tiny needles. The needles widen into thorns. I taste salt. I hold out my dripping palms to him, tears of ecstasy. I am saved.

Investigator: "My colleagues and I are nothing if not thorough and our examination of Benedetta Carlini and her claims was rigorous. She answered all of our questions in an articulate manner; her overall feeling was one of unworthiness and gratitude to the Lord for his gifts. The sudden appearance of Christ's wounds during our interview seemed completely genuine. The other nuns, especially her companion, Bartolomea Crivelli, corroborate her stories of trances, travails, receiving the stigmata, exchanging hearts with Christ. My colleagues and I left the interview satisfied that this woman was a true visionary."

Benedetta: Are you all right?

Bartolomea: Yes. Are you?

Benedetta: Yes. So…Were you frightened?

Bartolomea: The room was cold.

Benedetta: What did he ask you?

Bartolomea: He wanted to know what I had seen.

Benedetta: And you told him…

Bartolomea: Everything.

Benedetta: Everything?

Bartolomea: The truth. Is that not what you wanted?

Benedetta: Of course. And what did he say?

Bartolomea: He appeared pleased. He asked me to recount the events in more detail and then he dismissed me.

Benedetta: So…good. Good.

Bartolomea: You seem upset. Your forehead is bleeding…

Benedetta: Bartolomea…you did not tell him…EVERY-thing…about…

Bartolomea: The angel?

Benedetta: Yes.

Bartolomea: *Smiling.* He did not ask.

Benedetta: Of course not.

Bartolomea: I would not be able to explain it…the way you touch me, the way the angel touches me…he might think it was wrong.

Benedetta: He might.

Bartolomea: He does not understand.

Benedetta: No.

Professor: I don't give extensions for lesbian angst. I thought I made that policy very clear at the start of term.

Gwen: Extension? Who the hell needs an extension? I've got nothing but time on my hands, woman! That's the problem!

Professor: Oh, I see.

Gwen: I did the title page in CALLIGRAPHY. I picked just the right FONT. I bought special paper from KINKO'S.

Professor: Well, I'll look forward to that.

Gwen: It's not as if I haven't tried to procrastinate, okay, but every time I try to talk to her, she's mooning over a DEAD NUN. How can I compete with that? A dead pseudo-saint nun, man! Ya can't build on that! I don't understand why she can't see what's right in front of her face!

Professor: Maybe she's afraid of what's right in front of her face. Especially if it's right IN her face.

Gwen: Are you saying…

Professor: Maybe she just needs a little more time to work things through. To come to a decision.

Gwen: Come to a decision? Look at her SHOES for Christ's sake, she's COME to that decision!

Professor: Can I tell you a little story?

Gwen: Is a frog's ass water-tight?

Professor: One cold grey September morning, many years ago, a nineteen-year-old girl stepped off the bus from Thunder Bay to find herself in the great hairy metropolis of Toronto. Within hours of her arrival, following an urge that had been growing within her since childhood, she had shaved her head and gotten a tattoo of the Earth Mother of Willendorf. As the needles drove the last of the ink under her skin, she realized that in donning these outward trappings, she might be making a statement to the world about something that she herself was not yet ready to face. She was right—through her shorn head and a favourite pair of overalls, she found herself admitted to a tribe whose customs were alien to her, whose expectations were different from hers and whose tongues were pierced. She was welcomed, but continued to feel a sense of "otherness"— she retreated into books and learning. She took the time to identify her feelings and place them only in the context of herself. When she emerged from this cocoon, her hair was still pretty short, but she pierced her ears instead of her tongue to remind herself that while she may be associated with a tribe, she was first and foremost an individual.

Pause.

Gwen: You're from Thunder Bay?

Professor: Go talk to her.

Clare: I'm warning you, if you're here to mock me again, this crucifix is gonna…

Gwen: What? It's gonna what? 'cause whatever it is it's gonna do, Clare, it'll probably be the most action I've had in MONTHS.

Pause.

Gwen: You didn't come by to see me last night.

Clare: Oh, well…I was going to, but Nadia told me you were on a date.

Gwen: Oh, that's just great. Now even the FICTIONAL me is getting more action than the real me.

Clare: Nadia said you two were giggling and holding hands and stuff.

Gwen: Are you jealous?

Clare: Well, I…missed you…who was she?

Gwen: Okay, no, whoa, you were JEALOUS! You WERE, I can see it, oh geez, this is SO unfair. I spend weeks being jealous of your sick relationship with a four-hundred-year-old NUN and the one time YOU get jealous, it's because my sister came to take me for dinner.

Clare: Your sister.

Gwen: Yeah.

Clare: Was it good?

Gwen: It was okay.

Pause.

Gwen: Clare?

Clare: Mmmm?

Gwen: It can't have escaped your notice that I…well…that I've been, um, interested in…you know, you, and I think that maybe we…

Clare: I know.

Gwen: You know? You know what?

Clare: I mean, I know what you were going to say…

Gwen: You do.

Clare: Yes, I think so.

Gwen: And what was I going to say?

Clare: Aw, Gwen…

Gwen: Come on.

Clare: You were going to say that you…and I…that you think I'm…that we should…you know, try to…maybe…you know…

Gwen: Yeah, I know.

Pause.

Claire Frances Muir as Clare in *Benedetta Carlini*, NeXtFest 1996 (Photograph courtesy of Ian Jackson)

Gwen: Well, what do you think about that?

Clare: I'm…I don't know.

Gwen: Yeah. I know.

Pause. Gwen steps out of the scene.

Gwen: You know when you're watching a movie like, say, THE SOUND OF MUSIC where it starts out all cute and scrappy and charming and the threat of the Nazis is there but it's not really that big a deal until that point where it becomes clear that the family will have to leave and Rolf becomes a traitor and the next thing ya know it's "Edelweiss" 'til ya wanna puke and looking back in the film, you can see the precise moment—right after the marionnette show, in my opinion—where things start kinda suckin' and the whole thing just goes downhill? This is that moment.

Investigator: It was in the year of our Lord 1623 that I was once again called on by His Holiness to hold another investigation at the Theatine convent—Sister Benedetta Carlini, renowned mystic and now abbess of the convent, had apparently predicted her own death. On the appointed date, she died and was brought back to life a few hours later by her father confessor. Upon returning from the dead, she delivered messages to the congregation from Christ and the Blessed Virgin.

Gwen: Your problem, Clare, is that you don't want to watch 'til the end of the movie.

Professor: One of the things she told the people in attendance was that the Lord alone has the power to forgive and redeem His people and that the surest way to heaven was through direct supplication to God, rather than through the Church. This direct contact between Jesus, speaking through Benedetta, and the congregation made church officials VERY nervous; quite aside from the resurrection incident, here was a woman who claimed that Jesus was ignoring official church channels and speaking directly to the people through her. The position of the Church was precarious enough as it was without being challenged by an intelligent, ambitious, popular woman. All of a sudden, the Church wasn't too sweet on their new saint.

Investigator: Benedetta Carlini's death and resurrection posed a lot of questions, but as she was recovering from the experience, I began by questioning the other members of the order.

Professor: But it wasn't until the Church decided that she was verging on heresy that the nuns from the convent came forward to falsify her story.

Investigator: Sister Valentina reported having seen Sister Benedetta gouging holes in her palms with pins to make them bleed like the wounds of the stigmata. Sister Antonietta testified that she had seen Sister Benedetta painting on Christ's wedding ring with saffron dye and her own blood. Sister Carmelita reported having seen Sister Benedetta, who is on a strict diet of bread and water in order to ease the stomach troubles brought on by her travails, eating cheese and sausage late at night. Sister Genevieve, whose cell is next to that of Sister Benedetta and Sister Bartolomea, reported that she suspected something of a carnal nature to be going on between the abbess and her nurse.

Clare: Who's to say they were telling the truth? Who's to say they weren't simply jealous of her status and power? Who's to say the Church didn't put pressure on them to discredit her in order to save face?

Gwen: Who's to say they DID?

Bartolomea: I do not know the angel's name, but his voice is like honey and when he kisses me, I hold tight to his wings as he lifts me out of my body into the night sky. His face is her face and his hands are hers as well, but his voice is all his own, washing over me like water, sending shivers down my spine. When we are together, the curtain is drawn aside and I am filled with light.

I cannot tell this to the investigator.

To Benedetta. I cannot tell this to the investigator. He'll make it dirty, cover my hands with your blood.

Benedetta: Our blood.

Bartolomea: I love you. I cannot be the one who destroys you.

Benedetta: Whatever happens to me will not be your fault.

Bartolomea: I cannot bear to see your pain.

Benedetta: I love you too.

Bartolomea: I do not know what the others have said. I do not know if they have turned against her. I do not know what she has said. I cannot lie.

Investigator: Has she forced you to engage in sinful, lustful acts?

Bartolomea: She came to me as an angel, through the curtain. The angel is from God.

Clare: He does not understand.

Investigator: Has she corrupted you?

Pause.

Bartolomea: Yes.

Investigator: How?

Bartolomea: She…put her hands under me and corrupted me.

Investigator: Did she do this by force?

Bartolomea: I look up, because the answer is no. I see in his eyes that it is the wrong answer.

Investigator: Did she do this by force?

Bartolomea: Yes.

Benedetta: *Trance-like.* Hail Mary, full of grace, the Lord is with thee

It begins with my forehead. Tiny needles

Investigator: I confronted Benedetta Carlini with the accusations of her companion and the other nuns.

Bartolomea: I feel bile rising in my throat as I speak the word, my head hanging down, my veil touching my face gently…like her fingers on my face.

Benedetta: Blessed art thou among women and blessed is the fruit of thy womb, Jesus

The needles widen into thorns, piercing, penetrating

Investigator: She quickly renounced all of her former claims.

She confessed that anything she said or did was the fault of demons that possessed her.

Bartolomea: I lift my eyes to see the investigator, looking for an expression of horror, revulsion, pursed lips, tight fingers gripping his quill.

Benedetta: Holy Mary, Mother of God

The blood seeps from my forehead, just below the hairline, over my eyebrows, running down my face, filling my eyes with salt salt tears of bloody ecstasy

Investigator: Her repentence for having believed that the devil's work was God's was genuine and there did not seem to be any point in assigning her further penance.

Benedetta: Hail Mary, full of grace, the Lord is with thee

My palms start to itch, tingle, burn

Bartolomea: I look up and see him—and there is horror there, but also compassion.

Benedetta: The holes rip, the wounds widen

Investigator: She claimed that the visions had stopped and upon examination, her ring had disappeared and her wounds had healed.

Bartolomea: Compassion for me.

Benedetta: Holy Mary, Mother of God

The blood bursts forth, oozing sticky wound round my fingers, drips off their tips like fluid rubies

Investigator: She was nevertheless relieved of her position as abbess.

Bartolomea: Seduced by the devil.

Benedetta: My arms flung out, my head flung back

Investigator: One so weak cannot be trusted to lead a convent, especially in these troubled times.

Bartolomea: Weak woman.

Benedetta: The sound of metal hitting metal, dull dull clank, screaming echo

Investigator: I am satisfied that she will not fall prey to the Evil One again…

Bartolomea: My eyes fill with tears.

Benedetta: Metal stabbing, sudden, violent, hacking holes into my feet

Investigator: …and that the acts committed by herself and her companion, Bartolomea Crivelli, were contrivances of the devil for which neither woman can be blamed.

Bartolomea: My eyes fill with tears. He misreads them.

Benedetta: My side opens up and light spills out as my body lifts from my bed, blood spilling, running, oozing sticky, warm, salt salt, black, red, white light, white skin, white pain, my scream scream scream becomes a song of praise to the One to whom I have given my body, His face in shadow, He reaches out and wipes our blood from our face, and with His caress cradles me, cradles His child and says…and says…

Investigator: My child…

Bartolomea: I vomit.

Clare: I have tried over and over again to fill in the end of this story, but I can't. The words just will not come. I simply can't believe that she faked it all. I won't believe that.

Professor: The story of Benedetta Carlini is shrouded in mystery for the next forty years. No records exist of the investigator's pronouncements, and it is only the chance survival of a fragment of one nun's diary that allows us to know the outcome. On August 7, 1661, that nun, whose name has not come down to us, wrote in her diary: "Benedetta Carlini died at the age of 71 of fever and colic pains after eighteen days of illness. She died in penitence, having spent thirty-five years in prison."

Clare: Thirty-five years in prison, but a sentence administered five years after the Investigator had absolved her. How did she end up there? What…

Gwen: The yellow rubbery fuck HAPPENED? She DIED. She wasn't a martyr, Clare, she was a con artist. She was a woman who knew what she wanted, got greedy and got caught with her habit down around her knees.

Clare: She was a woman whose connection with her god threatened the already shaky hierarchical authority of the patriarchial post-Reformation Holy Roman Catholic and Apostolic Church! Don't you think that they would have gone to any lengths to silence her?

Gwen: That's not an argument, Mulder, that's paranoia. You're grasping at STRAWS here.

Clare: The Church was like the CIA back then, you know, they could have been plotting against her from the beginning— I mean, why would they be so scared of her if at least part of it wasn't true?

Gwen: Holy fuckin' mother of darkness, Clare, will you let this GO?

Clare: I CAN'T.

I need to believe in her.

Sometimes, Gwen, I think I'm the only person on earth who feels an irrational, desperate need to scream scream scream on a day to day basis. The scream starts small, quiet even, cuddled cozy in my gut until something triggers it— an event, a comment, a confrontation. And the soft gauze cradling the scream turns to stone as the scream ricochets around in its new walls, raging. It tosses bile into my throat, sets butterflies in my stomach, makes my knees go weak. The suppression nearly brings tears to my eyes, hold it in, hold it in. My hands shake with something I cannot even articulate. I have visions I can't describe, feelings I can't acknowledge...for fear the stone will crumble and I will not be able to stem the torrent of sound, words and not words.

I reach out across the ages to this woman, this sacred, holy, powerful woman, this woman who spoke the words of angels I don't believe exist.

She turns to Gwen.

Grip my hand. Send me your strength. I have no belief. Fill

me with your light. Help me because—the scream is getting harder to suppress.

Gwen reaches out to Clare. They go for the big embrace.

BLACKOUT

Sharla Matkin as Woman in *"No. Please–"*, NeXtFest 1996 (Photograph courtesy of Ian Jackson)

"NO. PLEASE—"

by Sean Callaghan

As his first play, *"No. Please–"* was a leaping-off point for Sean Callaghan, marking the beginning of his exploration of the modernization of communication and information, of population growth, and how these impact on human relations. "One of the strongest influences on me at the time," he writes, "was Lacan and his 'the world is a hall of mirrors' theory. So I wrote a play about a society or environment where the people have stretched so far away from any kind of self-recognition that they have inverted and become cannibalistic. What happens when one of them breaks out of the shell to see herself?"

For this he has created a rigidly regimented futuristic world where the retro '50s characters—he describes them as "cardboard cutouts"—begin to crack under the strain of the imposed conformity of an "antiseptic" authoritarian society (as in George Orwell's *1984*). Over the course of the play, facades crumble as husband, wife, and lover each give way to some degree of human passion, uncovering a three dimensional humanity beneath the two dimensional surface. This occurs the most distinctly in Woman. She decides to fulfill her own desires—indeed comes to realize that she has desires—and, fatally for her, begins to see herself reflected in the humanity around her.

Finding the right style and tone for the piece was a challenge in rehearsal. The play is not quite realism, nor completely science fiction; its tone is boldly comic as well as dark. Only when the director assigned each character something huge and impressionistic in the way of a costume piece did the actors feel as though they truly understood the play and their characters. Robert got a massive plastic flower for his lapel; Man, a massive toolbelt of a holster; and Woman a massive hair style and a large pair of shoes. Suddenly the actors felt they understood the world and style they were working in. Realism went out the window as they accepted the grand scale of emotion and risk beneath the surface. It became clear that when the characters stepped outside two dimensions, behaving with the passion and determination of full human beings, that their two dimensional world began to unravel.

Callaghan began his development of multimedia work in this play, which he further refined and explored in subsequent writing. In *"No. Please–"* he uses radio and television news to set the world of the play in context. At opening, we hear a radio news announcement listing train schedules, derailments, accidental deaths—all involving enormous numbers, all conveyed in a cool, detached style. In this way he sets up a world of massive population but little humanity. "The relationship between population growth and a person's sense of belonging struck me as strange," he notes. "That a person can feel more lonely the more people there are around just seems contrary to basic logic. So I wanted to stretch this idea out a bit. Test its boundaries."

The structure of *"No. Please–"* is more traditional than Callaghan's subsequent plays: *Opus 2. Karaoke Memories* (NeXtFest '98 mainstage and Edmonton Fringe, 1998) and *Masquerade* (workshopped at NeXtFest '97 and '98 and slated for production at NeXtFest '01). He has begun to combine other media with traditional theatrical conventions. By incorporating TV, video, internet, and film into these scripts, and characters communicating through screens and projections, he now works in a more interdisciplinary style. In his scrutiny of human relationships and communication in the contemporary world of multimedia that purport to project the "truth," he is asking who and what can we now actually trust to give us that "truth."

—G.S.

"No. Please—" was produced on the main stage of NeXtFest 1996, June 19-23 as follows:

Woman: *Sharla Matkin*
Robert: *Murray Utas*
Man: *Kevin Kruchkywich*

Director: *Kathryn Bracht*
Set: *Mariko Heidelk*
Costumes: *Lori-Lynn Pedersen*
Lighting: *Lori-Lynn Pedersen and Mariko Heidelk*
Stage Manager: *Glenda Stirling*

THE CHARACTERS

Woman: early to mid 20s, assembly line worker
Robert: late 20s, assembly line worker
Man: late 20s, police officer

THE SETTING

A train station and a dining/living room of a tiny apartment in the centre of a large metropolis.

NOTES ON SET DESIGN

The station is set with a bench downstage, the area darkened when not in use. The set for the apartment should be kept simple: dinner table with matching chairs, a small counter where the phone is kept, two exits—one to the kitchen and bedroom , the other to the outside—and a single tight little window looking out onto the blank face of another distant apartment complex. This is Man's palace. He is a tidy, repressed character. The set should reflect this.

"No. Please–"

Opening audio: People crowded on the platform of a train station. The buzz of hundreds of voices melting into one another creating a monotone drone of sound. The drone and all other sound is periodically overwhelmed by the sound of trains—massive mechanical beasts—roaring past the station.

Lights up.

A woman sits on a small seat in the station. She is the living image of the woman sitting in the cafe in Degas' "The Glass of Absinthe": lost and depressed. Her purse lies open at her feet, its contents spilled out beside her.

Enter Robert. He stands, waiting for his train. He sees Woman, recognizes her, attempts to say "Hello," but his greeting is drowned out by the sound of a passing train. Then, he notices her despairing expression and is overcome with sympathy for her. He stares at her compassionately an instant, then approaches, picking up the items spilled about her and placing them in her purse.

Robert: You dropped your purse.

Woman breaks from her depressed reverie and half listlessly grabs her purse.

Woman: Oh, thank you.

Woman looks up, sees Robert. Her expression changes immediately. Suddenly she is smiling and radiant.

Woman: Well, hello there!

Robert: I thought it was you.

Woman: Fancy meeting you outside of work.

Robert: Wonderful coincidence, isn't it?

Woman: Absolutely wonderful.

Robert: Going home?

Woman: Yes, I suppose. You?

Robert: Oh yes. Onto the K993, and home.

Woman: Oh.

Pause. Train approaches and passes.

Robert: *Voice drowned out.* You should be more careful with your things.

Woman: I'm sorry?

Robert: Pardon?

Woman: I didn't quite hear.

Robert: What's that?

Train fades away.

Woman: I didn't quite hear.

Robert: Oh, I said you should be more careful with your things.

Woman: My things?

Robert: Your purse.

Woman: Oh, of course. I don't know where my mind was.

Robert: You seemed distracted.

Woman: Off in some other place.

Robert: Some place nice, I hope. Some place exotic?

Woman: Oh no.

Robert: In the arms of your Italian lover, perhaps?

Woman: *Giggling.* Oh no.

Robert: Swedish lover, then?

Woman: *Laughing.* Oh no.

Robert: *Robustly.* The burly arms of a tall Spanish matador!

Woman: *Laughing uproariously.* Oh stop!

Robert: As he spins you around and around, his red cape flaring out like a tongue of flame.

Woman: Oh please stop! You're so silly! What an imagination!

Robert: No matador?

Woman: *Calming down.* Oh, you always know how to make me laugh.

Train passes.

Robert: *Tenderly, but drowned out.* I enjoy making you laugh.

Woman: Pardon me?

Robert: What?

Woman: What is that you said?

Robert leans in to hear better. Train fades.

Woman: What is that you said?

Robert pauses to think.

Robert: I've forgotten.

Woman: Oh.

Robert: Must not have been important.

Woman: No, I guess not.

Pause.

Robert: Well…it's been a pleasure.

Woman: You're going?

Robert: Yes, I'm afraid I must.

Woman: Oh.

Robert: Keep up the good cheer.

Woman: Thank you, I will.

Robert: Goodbye.

Woman: Goodbye.

Train approaches. Robert turns to go. Woman desperately reaches out and grabs his arm.

Woman: *Drowned out.* No, please don't go.

Robert: Pardon?

Trains passes and fades away.

Woman: I…

Robert: Are you all right?

Woman: Oh, I'm fine. Absolutely fine.

Robert: Are you sure?

Woman: Oh yes.

Robert: *Scrutinizes her closely.* You've been crying.

Woman: Have I?

Robert: Yes, you have.

Woman: *Touching her cheeks.* Well so I have! How awfully dreadful of me. So sorry.

Robert: That's quite all right.

Woman: *Examining her tears.* How peculiar. I must be out of sorts.

Robert: Out of sorts?

Woman: Nothing serious, I'm sure.

Robert hands her a tissue.

Woman: Oh, thank you.

Pause. Train passes.

Robert: *Tenderly, but drowned out.* Is there anything I can do?

Woman: I'm sorry?

Robert: *A little frustrated.* Can I help?

Woman: I can't hear you! The train!

Robert: What?

Train fades.

Woman: I didn't hear.

Robert: Oh. Never mind.

Pause.

Robert: You know what you need?

Woman: What's that?

Robert: A nice hot cup of cocoa.

Woman: You think?

Robert: Best thing in the world. Nothing better.

Woman: Nothing?

Robert: Absolutely nothing.

Woman: Well, then…

Robert: You should go straight home and have a nice cup of hot cocoa.

Woman: Yes, perhaps that's what I need.

Robert: I think so.

Woman: Well, then…

Robert: Yes…

Pause.

Robert: There's my train.

Woman: Is that it?

Robert: Yes. K993. That's it.

Woman: Well…

Robert: I guess I ought to be going.

Woman: Can't miss your train.

Robert: Hope you feel better soon.

Woman: Thank you.

Robert: Goodbye again.

Woman: Yes, goodbye.

Robert is about to go. Stops. Train pulls up.

Robert: I've just had a splendid idea.

Woman: Excuse me?

Robert: I've had a splendid idea.

Train stops.

Woman: I'm sorry. I didn't hear.

Robert: I said I just had a splendid idea.

Woman: What's that?

Robert: I know of a place that has excellent cocoa.

Woman: Really?

Robert: Not only that, something better than cocoa.

Woman: Better than cocoa? I thought there was nothing better than cocoa.

Robert: I was mistaken.

Woman: What could be better than cocoa?

Robert: Dancing.

Woman: Dancing!

Robert: Yes.

Woman: But it's still day! Who dances in the day?

Robert: I know a place.

Woman: Where?

Robert: Somewhere.

Woman: Oh please tell me.

Robert: I can't tell you. But I could show you.

Woman: Could you?

Robert: I could.

Woman: Oh, but your train!

Robert: Hm?

Woman: It's leaving!

Robert: Oh.

Both watch as train leaves.

Robert: Well, I suppose I can show you, now.

Woman: Splendid!

Robert: Though, it's quite out of the way. Do you have time?

Woman: I've the entire day to myself, and to be honest…

Robert: Yes?

Woman: I don't feel much like going home just yet.

Robert: Neither do I.

Woman: Well, then…

Robert: Shall we? *Offers his hand.*

Woman: Aren't we taking the train?

Robert: Oh no. The train doesn't go where we're going.

Woman: Oh.

Woman takes his hand. They exit.

SCENE 2

The living room of a tiny, one bedroom apartment. There is only enough room to accommodate a table, two chairs, a television, a shelf, and on the shelf, a radio, the remote control for the TV, and a phone. A small square window looking directly into the face of another massive apartment complex opens in the upstage left wall. A hall leads off stage left to the bedroom. Down from this is the door leading out of the apartment. A swinging door in the stage right wall leads to the kitchen.

The radio is on. Throughout the radio monologue, the moans and grunts of two people fucking can be heard from the off-stage bedroom. The scene opens with them both at the beginning of their rise to climax. As the radio monologue drones on, the grunts become wilder, more animal-like. When they reach climax, their voices drown the radio out in a terrible animal frenzy of sound.

Radio Announcer: It's seven thirty-three in the PM. You're listening to WDED Radio, 101.35 on the FM dial. Coming up immediately is RailManSix with the Metropol Rail Report.

Jingle: *Set to music.* One-oh-one-three-five W-D-E-D Radio.

Breathy Female Voice: Metropol Radio Report with RailManSix.

RailManSix: It's seven thirty-four, and this is RailManSix with the Metropol Radio Report. Derailment of the bee-three-five-three has left forty-five dead and seventy-six injured. Lines nine-fifty-five and two-thirty-five are closed for clean-up and repair. Estimated time of repair is two point seven hours. It's seven thirty-four. Derailment of the K-nine-twenty-seven leaves seventy-nine dead and only thirty-four injured. This closes line twenty-two. Estimated time of repair: three point zero hours. It's seven thirty-five. Collision of the A-A-two and M-C-forty-five closes line fifty-four, two-twenty-five and three. One hundred and forty-four dead. Five hundred and nineteen injured. Estimated time of repair is four point one hours. It's seven thirty-five. Here is the list of dead recorded as of seven twenty-nine today by the Metropol Rail Department of Surveys and Statistics: Arnold T. Abdulrazzak; Chun-li Abron; Friederich Adam; Donald Adamowicz...

At this point, the animal frenzy from the bedroom drowns out the radio.

...Boguslow, Carson; Daniel, Danilo; Joaquim, Lance; Marrila, Po Wan; Stacy, Tsui Ling, and Zamfir Adams; Nicolette D. Afaganis; Mario A. Agate; Horace W. Ahluwalia, Sr.; Jennifer K. Ahmed...

Frenzy dies down to silence.

...Wei Ching Akbar; Hashima, Maria; Robert and Wolfgang Akihiro; Jian Quan Alvarad; Suzanne Amlani; Ah Sobhi Anderson; Michelle Apostolakos; William B. Aramburu; Marcel Arbuthnott; Stephanie Ayoubianeshtehard; Kelly Aziz; Nhu Ban Babineau; Sarah W. Bach; Quang Ngoc Bailey...

Man enters from downstage left door carrying a large package of ground meat in his hands. He is of average looks and height, and he is balding slightly. He is wearing an official uniform. He appears well groomed and has a good humoured smile on his face. He moves to the radio on the shelf, dropping the package on the table en route. He turns off the radio.

Man: Hello-o.

No answer. He takes off his jacket, sets it on the back of the chair, pulls his gun from his holster and sets it on the table.

Woman: *Buttoning up her dress.* Hello dear. *Pecks Man on the cheek.* How was work?

Man: Fine. Fine. Were you sleeping?

Woman: Oh no. Actually I was with…

Enter Robert from bedroom, tucking in his shirt.

Man: Oh!

Woman: You don't mind, do you? I didn't think it would…

Man: *Keeping his good-humoured smile.* Why, of course not. *Reaching out his hand to Robert.* Hello. You're Robert, aren't you?

Robert: Yes. *Grasping offered hand.*

Man: I've heard so much about you.

Robert: Really?

Man: Oh yes! She never stops talking.

Robert: Well, don't believe a word. None of it's true.

All three laugh.

Man: She said you were funny.

Robert: She didn't.

Man: She did! She said, "That Robert, he's such a card."

Robert: You didn't!

Woman: You are! You always make me laugh.

Robert: Well, you're a bit of a hoot yourself.

Woman: Go on!

Robert: It's the truth. *To Man.* She's so modest.

Man: That's why I married her.

Robert: Good man.

Woman: Silly! You married me for love, remember. *Kisses Man on cheek.*

Man: *Wrapping arm around her waist.* Of course. For love!

Robert: Ah, *l'amore!*

They laugh.

Woman: *Indicating package.* This for dinner?

Man: There should be enough for tonight and tomorrow. Unless… *To Robert.* Will you be staying for dinner?

Robert: Oh no. I can't.

Woman: Oh yes. Please do.

Man: Please.

Robert: I'd love to, but really, I mustn't.

Man: Don't be silly.

Robert: I promised my wife I'd be home by nine.

Man: At least stay for a drink, then.

Robert: Really, you're too kind.

Man: Think nothing of it.

Woman: What would you like?

Robert: A beer is fine.

Woman: All right, two beer. *Exits to kitchen.*

Man: *Indicating chairs.* Please sit.

They sit.

Man: So…how was she?

Robert: Outstanding. Phenomenal. I doubt I've ever had the like.

Man: *Disconcerted.* Truly?

Robert: Stupendous!

Man: *Smiling again.* Yes, she is a pleasure.

Robert: You're a lucky man.

Man: *Leaning comfortably back on couch.* The luckiest.

Robert: Truly.

Man: I am the luckiest man I know!

Woman enters with two tall glasses of beer.

Woman: There you go, gentlemen.

Robert: Thank you.

Man: Thank you, dear.

Woman: *To Robert.* Are you sure you can't stay for dinner? There's more than enough.

Robert: I'm very sorry.

Woman: All right. *Exits to kitchen.*

Men take large gulps of beer, drinking till the glasses are half empty. Then both give a satisfied sigh and wipe their mouths clean.

Robert: You're an officer?

Man: That I am.

Robert: A noble profession. You must love it.

Man: I do. But, *sighs, picks up his gun, plays with the safety catch,* there are days…

Robert: Yes.

Man: Some days…

Robert: I can imagine.

Man: Like today.

Robert: Really?

Man: *Plays with the hammer of the gun, cocking and uncocking.* One nuisance after another. Honestly, by the end I wanted to shoot someone.

Robert: Terrible.

Man: They put the entire division on SS duty.

Robert: I'm sorry? "SS" duty?

Man: Oh, excuse me. It means "Street Sweep," for when we sweep the streets clean of the vermin, beggars, street people, drug addicts etc. etc. Terrible work.

Robert: I'm sure.

Man: But it must be done.

Robert: Of course.

Man: Messy, though. Very messy.

Robert: What…

Man: Yes?

Robert: Well…. What is done with the…with them?

Man: The vermin, you mean?

Robert: Yes. The vermin. How do you dispose of them? Are they sent away or locked up?

Man: Oh, nothing of the sort! We'd fill the prisons before lunch! No. It's the incinerator for most of them.

Robert: Oh, I see.

Man: Terrible waste if you ask me.

Robert: Yes, quite terrible.

Man: But there's nothing we can do.

Robert: Nothing?

Man: Usually they're so full of disease or alcohol or toxins, recycling them would be pointless!

Robert: Such a waste.

Man: The meat would never pass inspection.

Robert: Such a waste.

Man: Today we broke the record, you know. Twenty-five hundred and sixty-four bodies in four hours.

Robert: Amazing!

Man: Guess how many we were able to recycle.

Robert: I don't know.

Man: Go on. Guess.

Robert: Ummm…one thousand.

Man: Two hundred.

Robert: No!

Man: Two hundred!

Robert: Unbelievable.

Man: It was barely worth the effort of taking them to the plant.

Robert: I'm sure.

Man: The boys at the plant are always grateful, though.

Robert: So they should be.

Man: They gave each of us two kilos free of charge.

Robert: It's the least they could do.

Man: That package I brought in: two kilos of Prime A ground meat.

Robert: Really? Prime A!

Man: Doesn't come cheap. You're missing a fine meal.

Robert: I'm sorry to pass it up.

Man: *Long, luxurious sigh, gun still in hand.* Yes, it was a long day. I'm just glad to be home.

Robert: *Raising his glass.* To being home.

They clink glasses and down their drinks.

Pause.

Man: You're on the line with my wife.

Robert: It's not as noble as police work, but—

Man: Oh no! I admire you line workers.

Robert: You do?

Man: Oh yes! Working as a team. Depending one on the other to get the work done. It is the strongest and purest of human relationships.

Robert: Yes!

Man: Each man in a separate cubicle, yet working together towards a common goal.

Robert: I'm glad you appreciate it. So few people do. Some say it is lonely work.

Man: Not at all!

Robert: Some go insane, because they believe it is lonely work.

Man: All in their heads.

Robert: We've given them a name. "screamers" we call them, because once they start screaming...

Man and Robert: ...they never stop.

Man: Yes, we on the police force have to deal with them every day. We call them "sirens."

Robert: Five in the last week. Five screamers—or sirens. And just yesterday, it was the man in the stall next to mine.

Man: Terrible nuisance.

Robert: Just began screaming and screaming and wouldn't stop.

Man: Madness.

Robert: I had to break open the door and wrestle him to the ground.

Man: In my experience it's best just to shoot them.

Robert: I didn't have a gun.

Man: I've seen one pick up a man and throw him twenty feet.

Robert: He was a handful, but I managed.

Man: It's the adrenaline, I'm told.

Robert: You see, the trick is...let me show you.

Man: Pardon?

Robert: *Standing*. Stand up.

Man: Why?

Robert: I want to show you.

Man: Show me?

Robert: It's all right. It won't hurt.

Man: *Standing, smiling.* Of course not.

Robert: The trick is to get behind them, you see. But he, the screamer, was facing me so I had to grab him like so.

Before Man can react, Robert grabs his arm, twists it around his back and wraps his other arm around his neck. Man falls to his knees, red-

Murray Utas as Robert and Kevin Kruchkywich as Man in *"No. Please–"* at NeXtFest 1996 (Photograph courtesy of Ian Jackson)

faced. The gun has fallen just out of his reach.

Robert: You see, it's impossible to move. Try to break free.

Man struggles desperately, reaches for the gun.

Robert: Now, you're completely in my power. There's nothing you can do. One little squeeze and you're dusting your shoes at heaven's gate. You see?

Robert releases Man. Man quickly grabs gun and stands pointing the gun at Robert's face.

Robert: Ah! Now with a gun. There's nothing you can do against a gun. Except maybe—

Robert lunges and twists gun out of Man's hand.

Pause. Man smiles.

Man: Quite effective.

Robert: Ten years of martial arts. Comes in handy once in a while.

Man: Yes, well…

Man holds out his hand.

Robert: Oh, of course.

Robert hands Man back his gun. Man cocks hammer back.

Man: On the force, though, we usually don't have time to play games with an offender.

Robert: Of course not.

Man: An offender is a dangerous individual.

Robert: I know.

Man: He has no moral structure.

Robert: None whatsoever.

Man: He'll break into your home. Rape your wife. Steal your dignity. Steal everything that you're proud of, that makes you a man. Then, one night, while you're asleep, he'll sneak into your bedroom and slit your throat. An offender is not to be dealt with lightly. It's best just to shoot him. In the chest…

Man points gun at Robert's chest.

Man: …or between the eyes.

Man raises gun to Robert's eyes.

Man: My motto is "Shoot him when you can, before he invades your home."

Man squeezes trigger, the hammer snaps to, but the barrel is empty. He lowers gun.

Man: *Smiling.* Empty.

Robert: Yes, well…

Man takes box of bullets from shelf, begins to reload his gun.

Man: I'm just glad to be home.

Robert: And I should probably be getting back to mine.

Man: So soon?

Robert: Yes, I'm afraid. Thank you for the drink.

Man: You're welcome.

Robert: It's been…a pleasure.

Man: I'm sure it has. Come again.

Robert: I will.

Man: *Gun now completely reloaded.* Goodbye.

Robert: Goodbye.

Robert leaves. Man watches door close. He moves towards the kitchen, and stops outside the door.

Man: Honey!

Woman: *Entering.* Yes, dear? Oh! Where's Robert?

Man: Gone.

Woman: He left! He didn't even say goodbye.

Man: He said to say goodbye.

Woman: Oh…I was hoping he would stay for dinner. *Goes to window.* Maybe I can catch him on his way out. *Opens window, pokes her head out.* Oh, this window is so small, I can barely see anything. We might as well not have a window.

Man: Honey.

Woman continues to look out window.

Woman: I don't see him.

Man: Honey.

Woman: Hm?

Man: Close the window.

Woman: *Sighs.* I guess I could phone him later.

Woman closes the window.

Man: Honey.

Woman: Yes, dear?

Man: Come here.

Woman steps closer.

Man: Closer.

Woman: What?

Man: Closer.

Woman steps closer. Man grabs her, lifts her up onto the table, lifts up her skirt, begins undoing his pants. His actions are quick and methodical.

Woman: *Giggling.* Silly!

Man pulls her in closer.

Woman: Dinner's almost ready!

Man undoes her stockings. A bell rings from the kitchen.

Woman: There, see—it's ready… It'll burn, sweety!

Man stops, stares blankly at Woman. He then steps back and pulls up his pants. Woman leaps off the table and rushes into the kitchen. Man picks up remote control on shelf, sits, turns on TV. While Man watches, Woman enters, sets glasses on table, knives, forks, exits, enters with milk, sets it on table, exits.

TV News Reporter: …will begin enforcing mandatory sterilization in the new year. Downtown Los Angeles was the scene of another apartment bombing, the twenty-second this year. The devastating explosion destroyed the Monolith Apartment Complex and everything within a one-mile radius. Property damage is estimated to be between two to three billion dollars. Fatality is estimated at thirty-five hundred. Hurricane Damien continues its run over the southeastern coast. Winds of up to two hundred and sixty miles an hour have been recorded in Florida and Washington DC. All flights into and out of either states have been delayed as a result of the hurricane. Schedules should return to normal by the end of the weekend...

Woman enters with two plates in hand, each heaped with browned ground meat.

Woman: *Setting plates on table.* Two to three billion! How awful.

Man: *Switches off TV.* Yes.

Woman: Astonishing.

Man: Such a waste.

Woman: What kind of people would do such a thing?

Man: Maniacs. They should be shot.

Woman: Terrible.

Man begins shaking salt over his meal.

Woman: How was your day, dear?

Man: *Still shaking salt.* Was all right.

Woman: Oh? Mine was wonderful. We were let off early.

Man: *Still shaking salt.* Oh?

Woman: *Picks up milk carton, pours milk in Man's glass.* The battery shut down again, so they gave us the rest of the day off.

Man sets salt down, begins eating following a methodical pattern: one mouthful of food, one sip of milk, one mouthful of food, one sip of milk...

Woman: You know I spend all week all alone in that tight little box at work, and every minute I'm there I'm wishing I could be somewhere else, and then when I get a day off, suddenly I feel so lost. I swear, I didn't know what to do with myself. Luckily, I bumped into Bill Rogers. You remember Bill?

Man: Supervisor?

Woman: No. You're thinking of Bill Maxley.

Man: Swim instructor.

Woman: That's Bill Swain. Bill Rogers used to live in the Everest Complex just down the street. You met him once. He has the one eye.

Man grunts acknowledgment.

Woman: We had a lovely conversation. His wife's in the hospital, you know. *She's stopped eating.* I was going to go with him to visit her, but then we bumped into Joan on the B995 train. She had the most astonishing pair of shoes on…

Man: Joan Hansley?

Woman: Roberts. They were bright red and they had the most darling little pink bows. She was on her way to the modern engineering museum, and I sat there thinking to myself: "Do I want to go to the clinic to see Bill's wife"—who, by the way, is the strangest woman I've ever met, "or would I rather go to the museum with Joan?" After half a millisecond of consideration, I told Bill I wasn't feeling well and skipped onto the AA53 with Joan. I was so pleased with my decision, until Joan said the most hideous thing to me. I was commenting on how pretty her shoes were, and do you know what she said? Go on, guess.

Man: I haven't the foggiest notion.

Woman: She said: "Well, you know you can get them at Pauper's Paradise. I'm sure they'd have your size." My size! As if the size of my feet were so…abnormal! Well, I certainly was not going to sit there and let her insult me. Luckily, I saw Jane Dale in the next car, so as soon as the train stopped I zipped over to sit next to her.

Man: Hairstylist.

Woman: No, that's Jane Smiley.

Man: Manicurist.

Woman: Jane Cauley.

Man: Dietician?

Woman: Honestly! Janet Hanover.

Man: Jane Dale?

Woman: You've never met. She's new staff at work. She's in the stall across from me.

Man: Oh.

Woman: A nice woman I'm sure, but her voice. Dear me, her voice! I've heard dogs being skinned alive that sounded better. I could hardly stand it. Then I saw Gail Davies sitting on the PG67, so I hopped on it. Lucky for me I did, because later on I found out that the AA53 went and collided with the T90 not two stops from where I got off. I hope Jane's all right. I wonder if she'll make it to work tomorrow? At any rate, I went and said hello to Gail, but she's not the greatest of conversationalists and, besides, she has that horrible mole on her chin. So at the next stop I hopped onto the 9C9 and who do I find, but Arthur—Arthur Benhelm! But he was talking with Sally Freeson—whom I detest—so I wandered over to the next car and that's when I met Laura. Ah, Laura, Laura. What a darling creature. The kindest soul alive.

Man: Laura?

Pause.

Woman: Well, isn't that just awful of me. I don't remember her last name. Anyway, she had on the prettiest hat. It was black and trimmed with flowers—daisies, I think—and it had a long, black velvet ribbon wrapped round…Mansfield! That's her last name. Mansfield…I think. No matter. She was going to watch the digger's execution at The Gallow Stage, and I was so captivated by her hat that I just had to go with…

Man: You went to the diggers' execution?

Woman: Yes. The Gallow Stage was only a stop away and I…

Man: I heard they drew quite the crowd.

Woman: Who, dear?

Man: The diggers.

Woman: Yes. Everyone was there. Bob Mellman, Diane Kulowski, Dill, Rod and Mackey Anders…

Man: I was on the squad that brought them in.

Woman: Yes, I know, dear.

Man: We should've shot them right then and there.

Woman: Yes, dear.

Man: Sick creatures. Anarchists the lot of them. Talking about compassion and sympathy for the vermin. But I suppose they got what they deserved in the end. A clean execution?

Woman: Yes…well, almost.

Man: Yes?

Woman: There was a woman, she was the last to be hanged. She… *Suddenly gives her husband a confused look.*

Man: Yes, go on.

Woman: She was making quite the ruckus. It took two officials to keep her from…jumping off the stage. They had to tie her hands and feet together. Then when they were…I swear I don't know what's the matter with me. I'm all flushed.

Man: You were saying.

Woman: Oh, yes. When they were finally able to restrain her, she kept moving her head so they couldn't get the rope around her neck, and… *Again, the confused look.*

Man: Some of them can be quite the handful. I can't understand why they don't accept their punishment like decent human…

Woman: *Blurting out loudly.* No! It was quite comical. She made the crowd laugh.

Man: Well, if it was good entertainment, then.

Woman: Yes. She made everyone laugh. Then the most awkward thing happened. Someone... *confused look.*

Man: Honestly, dear. If you're going to tell the story, tell it.

Woman: I'm sorry. I simply don't know what's wrong with me. Where was I?

Man: An awkward thing happened.

Woman: *Stares blankly an instant.* Why, that's the most peculiar thing. I'm suddenly blank. I don't remember.

Man: You remember the execution.

Woman: Of course I do. They were hanged, but...

Man: Yes?

Woman: I'm sure there was something that happened just before...something was said...Why, how frightful. I must be losing my mind.

Man: *Scrutinizing her an instant.* Losing your mind. Ha! Ha!

Woman: *Smiling.* Honestly, dear. You're married to a mad-woman.

Man: Ha! Ha!

Woman: What a nuisance.

Man: What was said?

Woman: *Crinkling her brow in frustration.* Ohhhh!

Man: Who said it?

Woman: It was...Laura! Of course! It was Laura! Thank goodness. Thought I truly was going mad.

Man: What did she say?

Woman: Yes, now I remember. We were watching this poor girl making her valiant struggle to keep the rope from her neck, when Laura suddenly turned to me and said, "Why, dear! That girl looks just like you!" "Don't be silly," I told her. But then, everyone around agreed with her. "She's the splitting image," they said, and "You could be twins." I was so angry at Laura for saying such a thing and putting me in so awkward a position. I was ready to leave, but then I took a good long look at the girl and... *woman goes into a* *half trance, staring directly ahead of her.* It was amazing. She was right…

Man: That was very impolite of Laura.

Woman: …she looked just like me…

Man: To say such a thing.

Woman: …she was in a terrible state…

Man: Doesn't matter if she was right.

Woman: …but it was me…

Man: It's the principle of the thing.

Woman: There was a moment…

Man: Honestly, people like her ought to be shot.

Woman: *Breaking from her reverie, and suddenly snapping at Man.* What? What are you saying?

Man: I was saying how Laura should be more polite.

Woman: But I'm trying to tell you something.

Man: Yes, dear. The execution.

Woman: *Intensely.* Well stop interrupting me. Honestly, you go on and on about I don't know what! I don't care what you think! I'm talking now. *Calming down.* There was a moment …I was staring at this poor girl and suddenly she turned and looked right at me…and there was a moment when I felt…when I didn't know which eyes were mine, which face was mine…

Man: Are you ill?

Woman: She was so terrified.

Man: You look pale, dear.

Woman: But it was only for a moment, because then they dropped the doors and she fell…

Man: Something's wrong.

Woman: Snap! It happened so quickly. In a moment she was gone—not staring at anything at all.

Man: How do you feel?

Woman: *Snapping again.* What?

Man: You don't look well.

Woman: What is the matter with you?!

Man: You don't look well, at all.

Woman: *Gradually becoming irrational.* I'm fine! Fine! Fine! FINE!! What does it matter anyway? Aren't you listening? Don't you understand?

Man: Calm down, dear.

Woman: *Furious.* No, I will not calm down! This poor girl... Do you know what her last words were? I heard them. She was looking right at me, she said them right to me. "No. Please," she said. Two little words: "No. Please." Don't you see? Can't you see?

Man: I'm sorry I—

Woman: *In tears.* She was terrified! She was horrified by what was being done to her, and we all laughed. "Oh how funny! Oh look, she's struggling. How entertaining." I saw Laura— kind, good Laura—standing beside me laughing with the others and I wanted to knock that silly hat right off her head. That poor girl was terrified and all we could do was...

Pause.

Man: *Uncomfortable.* Yes, well...it is a tragedy, but justice had to be served. An example had to be made of them. What we let them get away with, we let a hundred others after them get away with.

Woman: *Slumping over in abandonment.* Yes, dear.

Man: Besides, they were maniacs. Not like you or me. Deviants. People like that don't think like you and I do.

Woman: More milk, dear?

Man: Yes, thank you.

Woman pours milk. Pause.

Man: Darling, you haven't touched your dinner.

Woman: *Looking at her plate.* Oh.

Man: Aren't you going to eat?

Woman: I'm not hungry.

Man grabs her plate, dumps meat onto his.

Man: I'm famished.

Pause.

Woman: How many people do you know?

Man: *Shaking salt over his plate.* Hm?

Woman: How many people do you know?

Man: What a peculiar question. I don't know. Many people. Hundreds? Thousands?

Woman: I don't mean people whose name you know or whose face you recognize. I mean, how many people do you honestly...know?

Man: Really, dear. I don't follow what you're...

Woman: I know no one.

Man: Now that's not true.

Woman: I talk to so many people. I see them everyday, and I don't know any of them.

Man: You're talking nonsense.

Woman: I don't even care enough about them to do them harm.

Man: Why would you want to do them harm?

Woman: I know no one, except maybe myself...

Man: You're ill. You should lie down.

Woman: ...and that girl.

Man: *Flustered.* All right, what on earth are you talking about? What girl? What's all this nonsense about?

Woman: Never mind. It's nothing, dear. *Rising, taking his plate.*

Are you finished?

Man: No!…No, I'm still eating.

Woman takes her empty plate into kitchen.

Woman: *Re-entering, smiling.* And Robert.

Man: Pardon?

Woman: I know Robert. We spent the whole day together. I met him in the station afterwards. It was wonderful. We went for a long walk, then we stopped at this curious little shop where I bought this wonderful dress. Don't you like it?

Man: Lovely, dear.

Woman: Then we went dancing. Can you imagine! Dancing in the daytime! It was so wonderful.

Man: I didn't think dance clubs were open during the day.

Woman: Oh, neither did I. But Robert knew this place down in the burrows where they dance all day and night.

Man: Down in the burrows!

Woman: Robert is such a wonderful dancer, too. He twirled me round and round the dance floor till I didn't know where I was.

Man: He took you to the burrows?

Woman: I could've been on another planet.

Man: The burrows are where we found the diggers. The burrows are where the vermin live.

Woman: Oh no. The people we met there were wonderful. So friendly.

Man: The entire place should be incinerated. That would solve our city's problems.

Woman: Oh dear! Ha! Ha! Don't be so silly! Ha! Ha!

Man: Where else did this Robert take you?

Woman: After dancing he was going to go, but it was still so early, even though I felt like we'd been dancing forever. You weren't going to be home for at least another hour, and you know I can't stand being alone that long, so I begged him to come home with me. All the way home we talked. Did you know he was afraid of going outside when he was young? Agoraphobia or claustrophobia, he said it was. He said every time he'd go outside he'd see all the tall buildings and all the people around him and he'd feel like he was standing in the mouth of some horrible beast that was going to swallow him up whole—so he would never go outside. He went to see doctors and psychologists and everything, but nothing helped. Finally, his parents dragged him kicking and screaming out of the building and told security not to let him back in until he got used to being outside. Three days and three nights they left him outside and finally he was cured. Isn't that interesting?

Man: Yes.

Woman: I thought it was the most adorable thing. I imagined him as a little boy terrified of all the tall buildings and I just had to hug him close. Then we went into the bedroom and I kept seeing this terrified little boy and I had to have him closer. I squeezed him tighter and tighter and then I put him inside me and… *sighing magnificently.* Ohh! It was ecstasy. Pure ecstasy.

Man stops eating to stare at Woman, who now stands staring out the window.

Woman: I think I'll have him over tomorrow. You know, this window is much too small. I can hardly see anything. *Opens window and sticks her head out.* Look at all the people. I wonder how many of them are afraid of tall buildings? Hello! HELLO DOWN THERE!! CAN ANYONE HEAR ME!?! CAN ANYONE—

Man picks up gun and shoots Woman. She falls to the ground. Man rises, walks over to her.

Woman: No. Please—

Man fires twice more. Woman is dead.

Lights up on stage train platform. Robert is standing as if listening for something or perhaps he'd just heard a noise.

Man moves to telephone, picks it up and dials.

Man: Hello? Daniel? Yes...I'm quite fine, thank you for asking. Listen, can you send someone to my apartment. I've had a bit of an incident, and I'll need help transporting the body to the plant.... A siren.... In my apartment.... Actually, it's my wife.... I don't know. One minute she was fine, the next she was screaming out the window.... Yes, and could you get him to bring the forms.... That's wonderful Daniel. Thank you very much.... You too. Goodbye.

Man hangs up phone, moves to window and closes it. Lights fade on room.

Robert hears nothing but the trains passing, gives up and sits on seat, full of despair.

BLACKOUT

Paul Matwychuk in *The Key to Violet's Apartment*, NeXtFest 1996 (Photograph courtesy of Ken Steer)

The Key to Violet's Apartment

a monologue by Paul Matwychuk

Paul Matwychuk's *The Key to Violet's Apartment* started life as two short stories. One is about two buddies attempting to understand what it's like to be a woman by carefully fabricating mind's eye versions of the kind of women they might like to be. The other is about the ubiquitous key to the apartment of a fey young woman whose character far transcends their ingenuous male constructs of woman and who may well be in the grip of strange fantasies about the men she knows. Matwychuk integrated these into a monologue exploring the ironies of gender expectation and the magic of "difference" in what has become his signature style of theatre. He tells "true" stories to the audience in the first person—his persona is "Paul"—with as little theatrical artifice as possible.

This playwright has taken an unusual road to playwriting. Discouraged in his attempts to publish the short stories he had written for his MA in CREATIVE WRITING at the University of Alberta, in 1995 Matwychuk decided to perform one of them at the Edmonton Fringe. This was a daring venture given that he had no theatre experience in performance, production, or writing. Without benefit of director or technical backup (beyond five sound cues), he rehearsed and performed his story, "The Muscular Stepmother," having tailored the text to his self-described "limitations as an actor."

His production succeeded quite well, but it took the encouragement of three theatre people to give him the confidence to continue: playwright David Belke with his generous review, and Ben Henderson and Bradley Moss who enjoyed his final performance and invited him to take part in the theatre festival they were organizing for the next summer. Consequently Paul brought his two stories to NeXtFest where he was encouraged to combine them into the play that became *The Key to Violet's Apartment* for the first New Play Cabaret. When Craddock's *SuperEd* coincidentally appeared on the same program, Matwychuk was temporarily discouraged: "Chris's amazing ability to play such a wide variety of characters in one piece made me doubt I was in the right profession—I can't even do accents—but Bradley and Ben convinced me to keep at it." Just as Craddock's training as an actor informs his writing, Matwychuk's training as a writer informs his presentation. Although he has now gone a step beyond straight story-telling in his use of dramaturges, directors and some set and lighting, his performances continue to emphasize story over virtuoso performance.

Matwychuk took *The Key to Violet's Apartment* to the 1996 Edmonton Fringe and returned to NeXtFest in 1997 with another monologue, *Hit The Road to Dreamland*, directed by Bradley Moss for the festival's main stage and then presented at the Edmonton Fringe. For NeXtFest '99, he once more teamed up with Bradley to attempt a five-character piece, "I See It," read at the New Play Cabaret but abandoned for another monologue, *Euripides Freakout*. NeXtFest playwright and director, Sophie Lees, directed this for the 1999 Edmonton Fringe. Matwychuk came full circle with his most recent production, *Lingerie*, at the 2000 Edmonton Fringe, directed by Ben Henderson—five years after Ben had invited the unknown short story writer to participate in the first festival. In Paul's own words:

> *What all this demonstrates, I think, is how welcoming and open the Edmonton theatre community is, even to completely unknown, absolutely raw writers and performers. The freewheeling, unpredictable marketplace of the Fringe is the most famous manifestation of this phenomenon, but NeXtFest, which is less high-pressure, less ruthless, and more consciously geared toward developing and nurturing young writers, is perhaps the best demonstration of how Edmonton theatre perpetuates itself.*

The Key to Violet's Apartment was first presented as a staged reading at the New Play Cabaret, NeXtFest 1996, June 19-23, performed by the playwright. It received its first full public performance at the Edmonton Fringe Theatre Festival in 1996, performed by Paul Matwychuk and stage managed by Sue Hopkirk.

PERFORMANCE NOTES

This play is performed with as little artifice as possible. Not only is the set kept to a minimum, but every attempt is made to convince the audience, however unbelievable the plot may seem, that this story actually happened. For instance, the name of the character in the script should be changed to the actor's name, and the actor might even walk onstage before the house lights go down. The tone for the first half of the play is very conversational with the actor feeling free to play off the audience's reactions to "Paul" and Max's little "what-if" session.

Once Violet's story begins, there is the sense that the actor is gradually assuming Violet's personality. Again, the transition is as "un-actor-ish" as possible—there is no need to make wholesale changes to voice or demeanor (certainly no suggestion of "drag"). At the same time, the actor's carriage is perceptibly different than before—more "feminine." Whereas the Paul/Max material is played with a certain awareness of the audience's reactions, the Violet story is a little more interior, as if Violet is sorting out these events more to herself than to any actual listener.

The Key to Violet's Apartment

Paul enters the stage, dressed in a sharp-looking suit. He is tall, bald and wears glasses. A leather desk chair is stage centre. Beside it is a small table bearing a pitcher of water and a glass tumbler. Paul ad-libs greetings to the audience, and then pours himself a glass of water, suddenly turning serious.

Paul: Everything I'm going to tell you over the next hour is true.

In 1955, the Ontario Court of Appeal decided the case of *Bell v. Bell.* This was something of a landmark decision in the history of family law—in it, the court had to decide which of two more or less equally qualified parents should be awarded custody of their young daughter. In the end, the court decided in favour of the mother, thereby helping to establish a precedent which would stand for decades afterwards. *Paul takes out a folded piece of paper from his pocket.* In his judgment, Mr. Justice Roach explained his reasoning in the following words:

Reading from the paper. And I quote: "No father, no matter how well-intentioned or how solicitous for the welfare of such a child, can take the full place of the mother. Instinctively, a little child, particularly a little girl, turns to her mother in her troubles, her doubts, and her fears. In that respect, nature seems to assert itself. The feminine touch means so much to a little girl; the frills and flounces and the ribbons in the manner of dress; the whispered consultations and confidences on matters which to the child's mind should only be discussed with Mother; the tender care, the soothing voice; all these things have a tremendous effect on the emotions of the child. This is nothing new; it is as old as human nature…."

Putting the paper away. Now, this passage has been used in modern classrooms and textbooks to help illustrate the sexism that still prevailed in the courtrooms of the '50s. But I don't think it *is* sexist, not really and truly, at least not in the pure sense of the word, that women are somehow an inferior class of people compared to men. Listen to Justice Roach's words. What came over him? It's practically an *ode* that he's written. This is one of the most remarkable and ecstatic passages ever committed to paper about the secret and mysterious power of women. I read it and I can tell—Justice Roach has come down with a kind of woman fever. He's practically in awe of them, but what goes on between them when the men aren't around, what secret and clandestine lessons mothers pass down to their daughters, what sacred trust is being brokered in those hushed whisperings—you imagine a close-up of a mother's red lips moving silently by her daughter's ear, a tiny ear, like a tiny seashell—he dares not even imagine. But he knows it's something beyond his ken, it's like breast milk or lullabies, and it's something a mere father couldn't *hope*, could not *dream*.... It's something he would never be able to provide.

And, you know, a friend told me that Albert *Camus* once made an observation about men—something to the effect that two men could be immersed in the deepest, most intellectual conversation imaginable, but that if a beautiful woman walked by, the conversation would halt while they both watched her pass. And I was very gratified to hear this, first of all, because this Camus comment sounded like something that Jerry *Seinfeld* might have said—you know, this was something even I could have come up with one of these days, and so maybe Camus' level of thought wasn't as far above me as I used to think. But, you know, the observation is still true despite that. It's just—okay, what are they really thinking of, the men in Camus' story, these brainy guys, when the knockout blonde saunters by, and I mean, she's twenty years old in a little skirt, and her name is Bernadette. Are they thinking of sex? Is that it? Or...are they thinking, pondering, about *women*? The frills and flounces. The ribbons in the manner of dress. The mystery. And not just eggheads, but you and me, when we see an attractive woman.

You see, I don't know. Because a month or so ago, I had the strangest day, and people were telling me the most extraordinary things, and now I'm not sure anymore about anything.

Paul sits down and takes a drink of water.

What it was, I was talking with my friend, Max. It was

Saturday, I was over at his place. My wife, Carol, and a friend of hers, Violet, were spending the afternoon shopping, sort of girls' day out, and I was watching a ballgame on TV with Max. But it was rained out, and so the TV was muted and we were talking instead. And the topic of the conversation wandered from this to that, and then Max started us down an interesting avenue.

We were sharing funny game-show stories. There was the one about the contestant on *The Price Is Right* who didn't notice that her breasts had popped out of her tube top while she was running down to Contestants' Row. There was the guy on *The Newlywed Game* who was asked to name the most unusual place he and his wife had ever had sex, and he answered, "Well, Bob, I guess that'd have to be in the butt." And there was the *Wheel of Fortune* champion who appeared on *Montel Williams* a week or two later to reveal that he or she or whatever, was actually a hermaphrodite. And there was the guy on *Family Feud* who, when he was asked to name the month when women begin to look pregnant, immediately answered, "September."

And we were laughing, and then Max leaned toward me with a look in his eye like Pepe Le Moko. And Max is an enormous guy, you know, really much too fat, with a terrible fat-guy beard that he neglects and lets scraggle way up to his cheekbones, and white socks with those cheap plastic sandals, and a baseball cap with his hair curled like a sombrero brim around the edges. And he leaned towards me and said, "That reminds me of a game show I saw once where they had ten boys from Grade Five. Ten-year-olds. And they were asking them a bunch of questions, but one of the questions they asked was, if you could be a girl for a day, just to see what it was like, would you do it?"

"Go on."

"Well, the idea was, the contestants had to guess how many of them would say yes. And…it turned out only one of them would admit to be, you know, willing to try it. And when the host asked the group which one it was, you know, for him to put up his hand…. Well, I mean, the looks the nine others gave him….I mean, sweet God, that kid was dead."

It seemed like the end of the story, and I laughed and reached for my beer on the coffee table. There was an ad playing on the TV for *V.I.P.*, the season finale, and I was looking at it while Max went on speaking.

He said, "*Poisonous* looks." He said, "I'll tell you, my heart went out to him, it really did. Sincerely, because, I mean, well, wouldn't *you* want to? Just for the experience? Wouldn't you?"

And I said, "Well, I don't know if I'd be up for that…"

And he almost leapt on me. "Oh, come on!" he says. Like I'm patently lying. He says he thinks the kid was just being honest! What kind of idiot *wouldn't* want to find out?

And I told Max I figured he was probably in the minority opinion on that, and he seemed almost wounded by how unenthusiastic I was being. I remember, we were sitting on opposite ends of his couch, and it was as if he floated across it, over these sky-blue pillows, and they were filthy, to where he was right next to me. And he was stroking his beard like Merlin the Magician and he said, "What— wouldn't you?"

Be a girl? A…a young lady? I tried to think of another funny game-show story, my mind racing, but that *Family Feud* anecdote was my last one, it was my funniest, and I'd saved it for last, and now I was empty! And then the word "Mademoiselle" floated briefly and tantalizingly through my mind, and I couldn't help but think what a musical word it was, and what a brilliant and absolutely perfect choice it was for the name of a fashion magazine.

And there was Max, moving in even closer. Saying, "Just for one day. One magical day. Just to see. Just to feel the world. Even for a short amount of time. Well? Well? Wouldn't you?"

And I was exasperated. "I don't know," I said. "Would *you*?" And I looked at him. His shirt—he had on a T-shirt he'd gotten free from a friend who worked for the Kokanee company and it was coming untucked at the side, exposing a white, hairy little oval of skin over his hip. And…and there was a corn chip stuck to the sleeve. He looked so hopelessly and foolishly masculine—he had to be aware of it. I think I thought he would see himself suddenly through my eyes, through the world's eyes. I thought he would, you know, realize his folly, if I can put it that way, and he would come to his senses. He'd have to answer no, and then the conversation could end. And then the rain would stop and the ballplayers could retake the field and we could be quiet and watch the game.

But instead, he just sat there with a grin on his face like something out of a pop-up book. He drew a woman in the air. He said, "*I* would. Like *that*." *Paul snaps his fingers.* And then he stood up and started pacing the floor like Vince Lombardi. He said, "I mean, don't you think that would be the greatest opportunity of your *life*? I mean, if you actually *could*? For free?! What…what kind of a…*rube* would refuse a bargain like that?" He seemed so incredulous that anyone could turn down such an…enticing offer…that I found myself wondering if saying yes mightn't be completely natural after all, and entirely acceptable. Maybe everyone would say yes. And then Max planted his feet in front of me and asked, as if for the final, final time, "Be honest with yourself. Wouldn't *you*?"

Fidgeting. "I don't know. Sure. I guess so."

"You *guess*? You *know* you would! In a heartbeat!" And he clapped his hands as if he were triumphant, and he sat back down and scratched his ass, and I thought at last, that was the end of it, but then Max turned off the TV with the remote, and he started in on me again. He sat right next to me, he was inches away from my face, like an anarchist in an animated cartoon, and he spoke in the deepest voice I'd ever heard him use, and he said, "Now then. What do you suppose you'd look like?"

And I just about rolled off the couch—you know: "Oh, for crying out loud, Max, *I* don't know!"

And he said how, well, I wasn't just going to look like myself! It was *infuriating* because I could tell he wasn't even joking about anything. He really wanted to know. What kind of a woman did I think I would be? He said I should try and choose, honestly choose, and he made an expansive gesture with his arm that seemed to include the entire world. He said, *imitating Max's gestures*, "Whatever your heart desires."

My heart's desire. That's a real…abracadabra of a phrase, and I think I actually felt something leap inside my chest when he used it, as if some enchanted organ I'd never known I even possessed were suddenly kicking into action.

"Now," Max said. "First of all. Are you going to be tall?"

And…I went along with him. I could tell he wasn't going to snicker or smile or sneer at anything I said, and I tried to imagine a comfortable height. "I guess…five-ten, five-eleven?" You know, I like being tall, and I figured that would be pretty tall for a woman, although…sometimes you see real Amazons walking around these days, six-three or even bigger, and I always fall in love with them immediately. Do you know what I say to myself when I see one of them? I say, "Together, we could sire a race of giants."

"Okay," Max said. "What colour hair would you want?"

And I said, "Hey! Wait a minute." You know, "What about you? You've got to choose, too!"

And Max, to his credit, answered me immediately. He said, "Okay, I'll be five-foot-three." Now, Max was something like six-foot-two, would be my guess, and like I say, a big, big guy, the kind of guy who gets nicknamed "Ox." And I wondered for a moment why he wanted to be so much shorter than he really was. He asked me what kind of hair I wanted to have, and I realized that, as a woman, I'd be half a foot taller than him, and I thought I could feel myself actually growing as I told him, I said, "Oh, I like blondes. I think I'd like to be a blonde. *Pause*. Oh! Um, down to my shoulders, I guess."

And Max kind of nodded and said, "Oh, so you can tie it back if you want, huh?" He said he'd want to be a redhead, either with very, very, very short hair, almost a crewcut, you know, like those artistic girls like to wear it, or else in a sort of a…what do you call this, where it's straight down to the cheekbones? Is that a pageboy?

I said I'd like to have blue eyes, and Max said he'd prefer green ones. We both would keep our fingernails short, but we each agreed that we'd get our ears pierced. And...I didn't say this at the time, but I think given half a chance, I'd probably get mine pierced three or four times each. I...I just went crazy.

And this is what men are like. Men are fetishists through and through, in a way that I don't think women can ever fully comprehend. Men have so many secret buttons—more "back doors" than any computer program ever invented—even they aren't aware of them. They just discover one day that, say, women's earlobes drive them crazy. You'll be able to name actresses with exactly the kind of earlobes you like—say, Ashley Judd and Sherilyn Fenn. Or it'll be that kind of aggressively fake, dyed red hair with the black roots clearly showing. Or whenever a woman wears those sandals—you know those sandals with the very thin sole and the straps that go up the calf and a separate loop just for the big toe?—whenever you see a woman wearing one of them, you'll go absolutely crazy with desire, you'll feel a yearning so deep it borders momentarily on pain, maybe not for her, exactly, but at least for the image of that foot...

So...pierced ears for me. I told Max that I would definitely have my ears pierced. And I mean, I hadn't been that sure about anything for a week. For a month and a *half*.

"Okay," Max said. "Um...what about the breasts?"

Now, I'd talked about breasts with Max many times before, and in fact, we'd been discussing them pretty animatedly just an hour earlier, but this was the first time I could remember myself actually blushing when the subject came up. Breasts...I wasn't sure if I wanted to have breasts...at all. And yet...I mean...I knew I'd need them.

Max was telling me to come on, this was one of the easier ones, and so I asked him what kind *he'd* want to have. He said he thought he'd want a small bust—he used the word "bust"—no larger than a 33B, say, and that was at the most. Now me.

I wondered at the time how many breasts I'd seen in my life. Actual, different breasts...I guess I was hoping that a pair I liked and would want to claim for myself would come on down the conveyor belt. I began counting them: there was Carol, that was two. Penelope, that was another two. Violet, Mary, Deborah, Tammy, two, two, two, two. I placed them back into my memory like animals being loaded onto the ark. Which ones should I choose? Should I make my own? I imagined sort of trying on each pair, what I could remember of them. From Penelope's, absolutely enormous, to Deborah's, barely there at all. Which were my favourites? Which choice would satisfy Max?

Finally, I just said 36C, which was really just a throwaway answer, but as soon as I said it, the kind of hazy female image I had in my mind seemed to lock into focus and complete itself and enter me. I could see her now, I could see her right there. I saw her legs and her face and her long, naked body, five-foot-eleven, and she seemed completely real and part of myself, even the breasts, and I thought for a moment I could even feel the weight of them pulling down on my chest. For only a moment.

Max was leaning back now on the couch, as if to better appraise me, like he was seeing the new me, my imaginary self. "All right.... What sort of figure would you want to have? Thin or fat?"

And I didn't need even to think anymore. "Oh, thin." And Max nodded and said, "Well, no one wants to be fat, do they? But, are we talking here like an athlete, or what?"

And I kind of surprised myself with my answer. I said I didn't think I'd want to be too athletic. I was picturing my old girlfriend Deborah's arms when I said it. Even today, even at this late date, they were still marvels to me. There wasn't a bit of fattiness or flab on them, and they weren't weak, but they weren't skinny either, or bumpy or at all muscular. They were…perfect, and delicate. They didn't seem to have a single bone inside them. And that's what I told Max I'd want to have. I said, "I think that's what I would like.... I wouldn't want to be fat, but I'd like there to be a kind of roundness to everything. That kind of thin roundness? Does that even make any sense? I can picture in my mind so clearly what I want, but putting it into words is hard, hard, hard."

I was almost talking under my breath, and Max was talking beside me too. He said, "Me, I'd kind of want a kind of athletic build. I'd want to be one of those short, lean...*capable* girls, you know?, with the pale skin and the dark glasses, dressed all in black, very aware, a little dangerous-looking. A little bit don't-fuck-with-me. I don't know what else I'd wear, though...I'm trying...I..." *Pause*. And his voice trailed off.

I didn't know what I'd wear, either. I didn't know much of anything about women's clothes, what the names of all the pieces were, the whole taxonomy of it, but, I mean, I'd seen women wearing things in the streets, and I started wondering what combinations would flatter me most. I did it. I pictured myself as a woman. Tall, taller than most, blonde, blue eyes, breasts soft and full...a wide mouth, a friendly smile. What did a skirt feel like to wear? Or, I'd always liked the look of those dresses that seemed to be popular four or five years ago, that ended in an abbreviated skirt but weren't tight, they were a thin material and they had colourful patterns printed on them. A girl in that REM video wore a black one with daisies on it. Holy smokes, it seemed so easy to picture myself as a woman that I wondered why I'd been so reluctant to play the game in the first place. And there was no shame or embarrassment to it, like in a...a transvestite fantasy, because I wouldn't be one. I'd be a woman through and through, and for only a day at most. Let's see...I'd need shoes if I was going to be a woman, black ones, flats because I'd be so tall, and I wasn't sure if I could manage heels, which are notoriously tricky to navigate in. And I couldn't decide what I'd wear to sleep at night. I couldn't choose between either a nightgown, even a satin or lace one, because why not, why not wear one after all; or a pair of oversize men's pyjamas, because I'd always found it so incredibly sexy when the women I knew put a pair of them on and let the sleeves flop over top of their hands. And I wondered... Would I even be able to sleep at all?

And then, suddenly, there was a woman's voice in the room—saying, "Hello? Hello?" And then there were two of them, going, "Hello? Anybody in?"

It was Carol and her friend, Violet. I could hear their shoes and their shopping bags rattling in the hallway. I opened my eyes, and I saw Max and I were sitting in the same position on the couch, leaning back and looking up at the ceiling with our eyes closed, like a pair of astronauts. I called out to Carol, "Um…we're in here, honey."

When she came in, Carol was carrying a heavy plastic bag and was slouching to one side with the weight of it. And Violet was behind her and when she saw Max and me sitting together on the couch, she got a kind of smirk on her face, as if she knew some sort of smart-alecky secret about the two of us. Carol kissed me on the top of my head, and saw that the TV was turned off, and she asked me if the game was over and I remember just muttering at her, just grunting, like, "Never started. Rain." For some reason, I'm speaking in these tiny sentences like I'm Ernest Hemingway.

And Carol was so *happy*! She lifted up her shopping bag for me to see and she said, "Did *I* ever do some shopping!"

I said that was good, and I said to Max that I guessed we were done here, huh? Max still hadn't shifted his position on the couch, he was still mulling the afternoon over, I guess. I said goodbye and still without really even looking at me, he gave me a kind of farewell G.I. salute.

Violet, Carol and I walked to the elevator, and when I reached over to carry Carol's bag for her, Violet laughed and called me "strongman."

On our way down together, Carol told me that she had told Violet that we'd give her a ride home, was that all right? And I said of course it was. Violet lived way the hell on the other side of the city, in, like, Castledowns, but I didn't mind. Violet was a good friend of ours, not just my wife's but mine as well, ever since university. I always had kind of a little crush on Violet. And she was dressed very attractively that afternoon. She was wearing a pair of sunglasses with these small, round lavender lenses, and her nails were painted that shade of red so deep that it practically looks black. And Carol was very chirpy and perky and all, and gee whiz, but as we pulled out of the parking lot behind Max's building, I kept sneaking one glance after another at Violet in the back seat of the car there in the rear-view mirror.

Violet. She was…something. Very pretty, but she kept herself…hidden away. A lot of people I know thought that—well, maybe not a lot, but a few, enough to make it a trend, and a lot of these were friends of Violet's, thought that she had a mean spirit. She liked to take small revenges, even for tiny, tiny slights, and she had a kind of an…icy soul. Now, I don't even know if Violet was aware she had this side to her—because I would see her, I would be there in the room with her, and I would watch her when she would…spill things accidentally on other people's important papers, or she'd just cause catastrophes by telling people things that she *knew* they were never meant to find out. And I would be there and I would watch her, and her face would turn as flat and blank as a porcelain mask when she did them. She just hid herself away.

And…she was a secret person in other ways. During the daytime, she always wore, like, work shirts and pants, no makeup, and her hair was cut fairly short and pulled into a pale ivory clip at the base of her neck. And you could just see her thinking, I'm not giving anything away for free, no one is getting any gifts from me. But at night, it was different, at night it was completely the reverse, because at night, she wore these elaborate white nightgowns, real Jean Harlow things, with that bright grey glow from the heavy, heavy satin, like an angel's outfit. She wore perfume in her hair. And I knew this, because I'd gone to her apartment unexpectedly early one morning—it was Saturday—because she'd borrowed a high-powered drill from me and I needed it back. I knocked on the door, and when she answered, she must have come straight out of bed, because there was this nightgown with the satin flying and banking all around her, and as I looked at her, all in white, with the drill in one hand and the smell of lilies coming out of her head, I was almost thunderstruck, I was so overcome that the truth just slipped out, and I told her, I said, "Violet…you're a vision this morning."

Carol was sitting beside me and she was leaning back

towards Violet and saying, "Come on! Come on! Tell us!
Tell us!" And I asked her what was going on, and she said
that Violet had a story she wanted to tell us once she had
us together, alone to herself. She said that Violet had had
her life changed.

And I said, "Oh, really?" I said it kind of mockingly, but
now that Carol mentioned it, Violet *did* look different that
afternoon, there was a gleeful expression on her face that I
couldn't remember ever having seen there before. Not icy
at all. And I suspected that this wasn't just hype on Carol
and Violet's part, that maybe something remarkable really
had happened to Violet and that she wanted to let us in on.

And Violet leaned back in the seat and she put her hand to
her forehead like this. *Paul demonstrates.* The car drove on
through the streets. It was drizzling out, the roads were
wet, and there was that continuously whishy sound underneath the tires. And Violet put her hand to her
forehead…and she began to tell her story.

She said, "I'll tell you the whole story because you're my
two closest friends in the entire world." And I was a little bit
shocked to hear that, because—well, not that I'd ever
thought about it before, but I'd always half-assumed that
surely there was *someone* who she was closer to than me.
And I decided then and there that she was lying…but I kept
listening all the same. She said, "First of all, I'd been having
these dreams lately. I dreamed that I was a woodpecker.
And I was flying around the neighbourhood where I used
to live when I was little. And I was going from tree to tree,
you know, and sucking out the sap and the bugs and all.
And—you know, where I live now, right? Well, there's this
apartment building about a block and a half away, that's,
like, so much better than mine, and…I could have moved
in there when I first came to Edmonton, but I was new in
town, and I was looking around, and I put it off and put it
off, and soon it was taken. And I can see that room—*my*
rightful room—from where I live now, and there's a couple
living in there, and they always have guests over. And
they've moved a goddamned grand *piano* in there, and the
guests all gather around it—and the husband plays it and
the wife sings. And it's enough to make you *sick*. And in my

dream, I flew across the courtyard and in through an open window, and I pecked the life out of them.

"And that's when I woke up," she said. "It was ten-thirty on a Wednesday morning. And I wasn't going in to work. I was just lying there, sort of mulling over the dream, you know, wondering what it might mean. And I just couldn't *think*. Dreams are just so impossible. So finally I got up. And there's this pair of satin slippers I like to wear in the mornings"—and here, she shot me a kind of hard-edged look in the rear-view—"and I swung my legs around, the slippers are always right in position there by the bed, and when I slid my foot in to the first of them, I realized that something was very, very wrong. There was water in my slipper, and I looked in the other one, and there was water in that one, too. They were full. And I looked up at the ceiling, but there weren't any leaks, and there wasn't any water anywhere else on the floor. So water, and it was cold, had somehow found its way into my morning slippers.

Paul takes off his glasses and, with a certain degree of understated cere-mony, places them on the table next to his chair. He takes a long drink of water, and then continues the story, assuming Violet's role.

"Well, I carried them to the bathroom and poured them out into the sink and I leaned against the vanity and looked at myself in the mirror, and I asked myself, What had hap-pened? Had I been sleepwalking? Where had the water come from? And I turned around and leaned back against the vanity and looked across my apartment, over at my bed and the window above it. It was…a beautiful morning out-side. There were these thin white clouds, and a blue, blue sky and just…oh, tree after tree along the sidewalks.

"You know, this is the first time I've told this story to anyone.

"Well, I showered, and I remember, I just kept drying myself, fanatically, like I couldn't stop. It was as if an air of mystery had spread itself out through my apartment, like a fog. The place was absolutely *humid* with mystery. I hung the slippers up to dry, and there were dark patches where the water had started to seep through.

"I got dressed and I was about to go out, when I went to the closet by the front door. I had something like twelve pairs of shoes in there, and ordinarily, I just threw them inside, like in a pile, but now, they were arranged in these same, precise rows, and *they* had been filled with water, too. I have this pair of thigh-high boots, and they had these metal rods inside them to keep them upright, and they were filled to the brim. And my high heels were all full, and my running shoes were full. And I didn't own any sandals—I don't know *what* would have happened if I had. And I was running around the apartment, you know, and there was even this pair of moccasins that I'd thrown underneath the bed, like, six months ago, and they'd been filled with water, too. I was crouching down and lifting up the bedspread, and you could see the light shining on the surface of the water, like a pair of underground lakes. Like a miniature grotto.

"Well, I went to the front door, and there was part of the mystery solved right there, because the door was unlocked, and I *remembered*, the night before, I'd gone to bed, and I'd forgotten to lock the door. I hadn't even pressed the button in the knob, you know, let alone slide the chain. It was so spooky—it was the middle of the morning, but I could see things as if it were the middle of the night...the knob turning in the dark, the moon reflecting off the metal, and the door is opening slowly...and there's a shadowy figure on the other side...waiting to enter. *Paul shudders involuntarily, and then regains control of himself.*

"So, anyway, there was this whole operation where I had to find a bucket and empty all the shoes, all the water into it, and carry it back to the kitchen and dump it out, and, I mean, I needed to make, like, *three* trips to get rid of it all. Up and down the hallway. And while I was doing that, I saw this bracelet of mine, a gold bracelet, lying on top of a table, in plain view. And I realized that nothing I owned seemed to be missing. And I checked, I looked through my drawers, none of my jewelry had been taken. And last week, I'd found $200 in a money clip on a park bench and I'd taken it home and hidden it inside a hatbox on the top shelf of my closet, and I looked, and it hadn't been taken, either. The box hadn't even been opened. And none of my doors were ajar, and nothing I owned was out of place. So whoever had done this—and I realized now that someone had been in my apartment last night—whoever had crawled around my rooms for hours, for the better part of the night, hadn't disturbed a thing. He'd left everything just the way it was.

"And, I mean, it could've been anyone. And I had this vision, of the entire apartment with this *swarm* of mysterious people inside, with…cloaks, and penlight flashlights, watering all my plants and ladling out soup into all my bowls. But then I realized, it *couldn't* have been *anyone*—it wasn't some thief, he hadn't *taken* anything. And I realized, with a start, that it must have been someone I knew! Like, a friend, or someone I'd met before. He knew my apartment, he knew it exactly. I must have invited him in some time ago, and, and, I might have fed him or entertained him, and he'd come back—what? A month, two months, a *year* later? In the middle of the night and he'd tried to play a joke on me. But what was the joke? I didn't understand. What was it all supposed to mean?

"Well, I asked around the neighbours if they'd seen anybody going into or leaving my place last night, but none of them had. And I mean, I'd fallen asleep around one AM, and I'd woken up at ten-thirty, which was, like, nine hours, and no one could give me a single clue. And I called some friends and asked them if they knew anything about anybody planning a prank on me, but that didn't turn up anything, either. And I knew better than to call the police and trying to explain the situation to *them*. It was just, so *impossible*. And I remembered suddenly that two weeks ago, I'd gotten two guys fired at work—they'd stolen about $5,000, and I knew it. I'd written an anonymous note tipping the company off. And I thought maybe it was them, they'd found out somehow it was me, and they'd tried to wreak their revenge. And I could picture them, Gregory and Hal, outside my apartment in the middle of the night, working a hairpin into the lock and then smiling at each other because the door was open already. But…this wasn't revenge. I didn't know what this was. And I realized, as I thought back over all the parties I'd ever thrown at my apartment, that neither Gregory nor Hal had ever been inside it before.

Pause. "Well, the next morning I got a phone call. It was Henry—you know Henry, right? From Brazil? And I'd called him the day before to ask if he knew anything about the water trick, and he said then that he didn't have a clue what I was talking about, but then he said he had something urgent, something terribly, terribly urgent that he wanted to tell me, and we made a date to meet for lunch.

"It was in this restaurant, and he had us sit way in the back, in this jungly corner, behind these potted rubber plants, and he said he had a confession he had to make to me. About three years ago, I'd gone out east to Nova Scotia to visit my parents, and I'd asked Henry to look after my apartment for me. I needed someone to look after my birds. You remember how I used to have a pair of lovebirds in a brass cage in my kitchen? I'd asked Henry to feed my birds and collect my mail, and water my African violets. And I'd given him a copy of the key to my apartment. And that was what he said he had to make his confession about. The key.

"He said…that he'd made a copy of the duplicate, and he'd kept it for himself. And he insisted that he hadn't ever used it or anything, but that he'd loaned it once to a friend of his, Edward. And now, all I knew about Edward was that he had red hair and Henry used to play tennis with him all the time, but Henry said that Edward was in love with me. He said Edward knew a florist named Murchison, if you can believe it, and together, they were going to fill a room with roses for me and leave a beautiful love note at the bottom of the pile. And Henry was going to help them. He was going to watch my apartment and wait until I'd left for work, and it was safe, and he'd notify them, and then they'd drive the florist van around back of the building, and carry all the roses up to my room and surprise me when I got home.

"And I said, 'But Henry…. What happened? I never got any roses.'

"And Henry said…that Edward had left town before the plan could take place. He left on a luxury airplane, and when Henry last spoke to him, he wasn't making any plans to come back. He had a job now, in Boston, with Singer Sewing Machines and Henry said he'd fallen out of love with me, like a hysteria that's passed. He said that once he couldn't get me out of his mind but that now…well, now he could.

"And I stared at Henry. I could have murdered him. I could have stabbed a fork in his eye. I kept saying to him, 'My key, you gave away my key.' And he kept apologizing, and spreading his hands out like this, but I just shouted at him louder than ever, until he wound up slamming his hands onto the table and pointing at the exit and *ordering* me away from his table. And I left, but before I did, I told him how much I hated him, and how I never wanted to see him again, for as long as I lived.

"I left the restaurant in a kind of daze. I didn't know if Edward was still a suspect or not. Such elaborate plans he'd made, and how simply and easily he'd called them all off, and I wondered if I'd done something, if maybe he'd seen me do something so completely unlovable that he'd been left with no other choice, and I thought immediately of the $200 in my hatbox. But then I realized that Henry's story wasn't even a clue—so *what* if Edward had a key? What difference did *that* make? The door was open. I'd—I'd practically invited *anybody* to come in.

"Now, I know this woman named Mary. She's a bartender, and the last Thursday of every month we get together and talk about life. We used to live together, did you know that? And we used to *fight*…pulling hair, clawing—you know, women know how to really *brawl*. They don't play by any stupid rules. Once, she caught me talking on the phone with Bradley, and she cut the cord in two with a carving knife, and then I just went after her with a high-powered drill we had lying around. Unbelievable! But the funny thing was, after we moved out on each other, we just became the best of friends, we were like sisters, we were like something out of a long distance commercial, and we got together every month and told each other secrets. And that night, it was one of our Thursdays, Mary told me a big one.

"She didn't know anything about anybody sneaking into my apartment, and she'd said as much when I called her on Wednesday, but she *did* know something about Henry. She…she knew a lot of things, though. She knows about secret conversations taking place in the dark, in the middle of the night, between people who believe they're entirely unobserved. She's...she's tiny—men can pick her up and carry her around. And she cries at everything—she cries at, like, greeting cards. And she knows how to piece together connections between people who are pretending that they're meeting for the very first time, letting on they've never laid eyes on each other before.

"And she knew about Henry. She said that Henry had never done a bad thing in his life, or at least nothing mean. When he was nine years old, he used to save up his allowance and buy these jumbo chocolate bars. He'd wrap them up in paper, and put them in people's mailboxes, put them in *strangers'*, you understand, and he'd ring the doorbell and run away. And now he was, you know, a full-grown man, Brazilian, with this beautiful skin, and musclebound, forearms like, like Popeye, and to look at him, you'd hardly expect him to be...any source of kindness. He surprised you. But he'd done a dumb thing, Mary said. He'd confided his deepest secret to her one evening after they'd gone to see a very depressing play. He'd taken her to the restaurant with the potted rubber plants, and he told her...he told her he hadn't just made *one* copy of the key to my apartment. He'd made dozens, and he used to give them away to his friends. And he swore up and down that he never told them what door it was that they opened, that was a sacred, sacred secret—he meant them more as a symbol of friendship instead.

"Mary's story went like this:

"Henry made his living designing furniture. And that's how I first met him—I'd hired him to build a special cabinet for my bedroom. And Mary said when I started arguing with him over the price he wanted to charge me, he just became smitten with me. Lovesick! And I remembered it now, I remembered it properly, we met for lunch to go over the numbers, and he wound up conceding on every point. He put aside prior deadlines so he could lavish even more attention on *my* project. He—he built his entire day, Mary told me, around the hour when I'd come by his workshop to check on his progress. And once...oooohhh... *memory dawning.* Once, he tried to hold my hand, but I wouldn't even let him do that. *Paul winces and makes a gesture of regret and sorrow.* I mean…you know how I am. And he was so impossible. But…I mean, we still met and talked with each other and had lunch, long after he'd finished the cabinet, and Mary said Henry felt we had a special rapport, a secret connection of the souls. He was Brazilian, he could be very mystical about these things. And three years ago, Henry took the key I'd given him to my apartment down to his workshop, just to make a copy, just in case, but he found, after he'd finished making the first one, that he was entirely unable to stop.

"And Mary wouldn't stop, either. I told her how it bowled me over, how astonished I was to learn that Henry had a crush on me, and that, even after everything that had happened, after all these years, he might have one yet. And Mary said it didn't end there, and she reeled off an entire…*litany* of names of people who had felt the same way about me over the past six months alone. Andy was in love with me, she said, and Leon, and a second Edward, and a teenaged boy named Gordie, and Bradley! Bradley! And all along I'd thought he was in love with my old friend Beth! Mary said Marty was in love with me, and Steve, and Isaac, and Oliver, and a lesbian sculptor named Sandra. An absolute *ocean* of admirers. Teeming around me.

Sighs. "And when I got home that night, well, I felt dizzy. I felt *seasick.* On the one hand, I'd lost so many things over the last couple of days. I'd snagged a button on a railing when I was leaving the building one morning, and it was an antique, it was made of greenglass, and now it was gone. And I'd lost the $200 in my hatbox—I'd put it into an envelope before I went to the restaurant with Henry, and I had it with me when I got up to leave, but by the time I'd gotten back home, I could feel inside my pocket and tell that it had vanished, and I hadn't even stopped anywhere along the way. And I'd lost Edward…two years ago, but I was only finding out about it now. But on the other hand, there were presents I'd received, too. Back at the restaurant with Henry, I'd ordered dessert, and someone in the kitchen must have goofed, because it arrived with extra cream and twice as much filling as it was supposed to have. And there was Mary's list of names. And I supposed that you could even look at all the water in my shoes that morning as a strange kind of gift as well. If you wanted to.

"But who had given it to me? Was it maybe Edward? Back from Boston? I guess it could have been…I mean, planes made the trip all the time. But I really suspected Henry, the obvious one, ahead of everybody else. And that night, I had an insight, like a psychic flash. It was another dream. I dreamed that Henry had returned to my apartment at three o'clock in the morning. He had a keyring with him the size of a dinner plate. He slipped one of the keys into my door and it opened without its making a sound. He dropped immediately to the floor, and I could see him now, I could see him right there. And I decided then that I could love him, that it was Henry, out of all the suspects, who was the culprit from the start. I watched him as he opened the closet door to the right of him and began pouring water into all my shoes. With all the care he could muster. One more time. He had a canteen with him, and I remember thinking, oh no, I could tell it was emptying, it wouldn't hold enough, where would the rest of the water come from? And then…I saw…that he had three, four canteens strapped to his back. My heart almost stopped. He loved me so much he needed four canteens to finish the job."

Paul looks at the audience a little sheepishly, and then sits back on his chair. After a short pause, he puts his glasses back on, and drains the rest of the glass of water in one long draught. He then continues the rest of the story as himself.

We'd arrived at Violet's apartment about five minutes before, but I just parked in front of the building and left the engine running while she finished her story. When it was over, Violet sort of grinned at Carol and me and said, "I guess it's a pretty wild tale, huh?" Then she got out of the car and ran up the steps to her building and disappeared into the lobby. Carol and I sat there silently for a few moments until finally I said, "Do you believe a word of what she just told us?" And Carol said of course she did, as if I were being perverse for even doubting it, and when I asked her how she could be so sure, she just said, "Because it all sounded so real."

We were pretty silent as we drove back home. At one point, we stopped at a traffic light, and a teenaged girl in a prom dress crossed the street in front of us. Her dress was a deep royal blue and her shoes had been dyed to match it. There was a white and pink corsage on her wrist on a ribbon, and around her neck was a locket the shape of a swollen silvery heart. It was freezing outside, with the drizzle, and I wondered how cold she was, I wondered if the hairs on her arm were prickling. There were some friends of hers waiting for her underneath the awning of a hotel, and I watched her cross the street and kiss one of them on the cheek. I missed the light turning green, I just thought she looked...*hopeless sigh*...so young and beautiful.

A little while later, Carol asked me what Max and I had been talking about when she and Violet had come into the room, and I said, "Oh, nothing. Well—we'd just been talking... um, Max was asking, if you could be a woman for a day or two, just to see what it was like, whether you'd do it."

And Carol laughed and said, "A day or two? You'd have to spend the entire *month* as a woman to really see what it's like."

And I marvelled at her comment. A month? What would I do with a whole *month* as a woman? I'd have to buy an entire wardrobe if it was going to be a month. All the stores I'd have to visit....A month! For some reason, I imagined Carol completely out of my new life. I saw myself renting an entirely different apartment, somewhere near the river. It had bare wooden floors, cool against your feet in the morning. I didn't even imagine myself having a job. Instead, I found myself wondering if I'd meet anyone that month. I wondered if I'd meet a man, if I'd actually go out with a man. Or would I just naturally gravitate towards women again? These were honest questions. I wondered if maybe I'd look up Max, short, redheaded Max with the athletic build and the tiny bust, and if maybe something would happen between us? What would *that* be like? And suddenly, I had no idea. I looked at Carol sitting in the car beside me, with her knees close together, and her bare legs crossed at the ankles. I didn't know *what* it would feel like. I wanted nothing to do with men the way I was now, but somehow, if I thought of myself during that hypothetical month, it didn't seem to matter whether it was a man or a woman I got myself entangled with. All I knew was that I thought it would be incredibly different.

Pause. That night, Carol and I made love.

It was the middle of the night, and I couldn't sleep, and the moon was in the window. I was listening to Carol breathing. It was shallow, with a faint whistle in it, and I rolled over onto my side to be closer to it. The sheets moved up and down with each breath she took. Soon, very quietly, with all the care I could muster, I reached underneath the T-shirt she was wearing and I put my hand on her breast. It rose and fell, infinitely soft and shapeless and mysterious beneath my hand.

Soon, Carol rolled over with a little moan to kiss me, but I couldn't be sure if she was awake yet or not. She put her arms around me and she made these little noises of pleasure, but her eyes were still closed and she moved, I thought, with the underwater slowness of a dreamer.

Now, I'd never thought of Carol before as mysterious, and in fact, that was probably partly why I'd married her in the first place, because she seemed so knowable and reliable and trustworthy. But now, as I moved on top of her and bit at her neck and her ears, I wondered. Carol was moving beneath me now, in cooperation, and her face had a wide, almost liquid smile of delight across it. I was as excited as ever, but as excited as I was, my mind was still clear. I still knew exactly who I was and precisely where and just what I was doing. But Carol....Carol had locked her legs around my back and I thought as I looked at her face and her smile with one tooth biting into it that she seemed to be going almost insane, almost driven outside herself and far, far away with the sheer pleasure of it all. And suddenly, there seemed to be no drawbacks, nothing undesirable at all, in the world of women, I said it to myself over and over again, the thought washed over me in great, soft, sea-blue waves, *nothing* that wasn't wonderfully, *wonderfully*...different.

BLACKOUT

Tuesdays and Sundays

by Daniel Arnold with Medina Hahn

Tuesdays and Sundays is based on an actual love story that took place on Prince Edward Island in 1887. As poetically recreated by Daniel Arnold and Medina Hahn, the play effectively creates two worlds, the limbo in which young William and Mary awaken at opening, and the rural community of Margate where they met and fell in love in 1887. The two worlds are not wholly separate, however. Through language and memory, the pair recreate their courtship in an economical blend of poignancy and humour while still in the dream or limbo state which could be one day, or one hundred years, after their story ended.

Arnold and Hahn had worked together as classmates in the BFA acting program at the University of Alberta, from which they graduated in 2000. Early in their student days they talked of producing a show in which they both would perform, recognizing the importance of creating their own work because, "You can't always depend on other people to hire you."

At NeXtFest '99 (where he performed in *lightergame*) and the Edmonton Fringe that year, Daniel was inspired to create a show himself by such plays as *Stale Mate, Crave*, and *The Drowning Girls,* chiefly because of their use of language and simple theatricality to tell a good story. The two had begun searching for their own story when Daniel came across the tale of William Millman and Mary Tuplin in several Canadian true crime collections. He began reading trial testimony, eye witness accounts, and comments of local people at the time of the events of the play. The setting, names, year, and facts of actual events remain the same, but the creators also wanted to give their own interpretation: "The emotional truth between the actual couple will never be known, so we wrote one possibility."

When they began working on *Tuesdays and Sundays*, they had no idea just how collaborative it would be. Originally Daniel intended to write the play alone. However, they soon discovered that Medina's contributions went beyond the mere reading of early drafts. Daniel describes the collaborative process: "I would write, then we'd read it together. I'd write some more, and we would read again. Medina would ask questions, edit, give new ideas, provide answers and inspiration, and I would continue to write." Or as Medina remembers, "I would say, 'I wouldn't say it like that. I'd say it like this…'"

During their final year in Acting, Daniel received funding from the Alberta Foundation for the Arts to further develop *Tuesdays and Sundays*, which, he says, "spurred on our collaboration and provided us with a deadline." At the very last minute they completed a draft for submission to NeXtFest. Festival dramaturge Wojtek Kozlinski so admired the play's potential that he took the unprecedented step of directing the play to ensure that no other director would "muck up" its beautiful language with elaborate and unnecessarily complicated staging and sets. In Daniel's words, "His influence was phenomenal. Over the next month we saw a number of drafts in which the style and characterization became clearer and distilled." Anachronisms of speech were expunged, the language was kept simple, some facts were changed to satisfy the demands of theatricality, and the articulation of images began. Within weeks the script was refined and rehearsed, and the simple, evocative set evolved.

At NeXtFest, the play received standing ovations at every performance, and continued on to production in the 2000 Edmonton Fringe Festival. The collaborators attribute the play's success entirely to NeXtFest. "It provided us with a schedule, venue, funding, advertising, rehearsal space, artistic and technical team, and a fantastic director/dramaturge. Most importantly NeXtFest provided an audience for William and Mary."

—G.S.

Tuesdays and Sundays was originally produced at Theatre Network's NeXtFest in the Roxy Theatre from June 6-11, 2000, as follows:

CAST

William: *Daniel Arnold*
Mary: *Medina Hahn*

Director/ Dramaturge: *Wojtek Kozlinski*
Designer: *Catherine Mudryk*
Stage Manager: *Andrew Brooks*

CHARACTERS

William: an eighteen-year-old farm boy
Mary: a sixteen-year-old farm girl

SETTING

A memory of Margate, 1887

PRODUCTION NOTE

The original set was minimal and abstract. It consisted of a small raised platform and some stepping-stones on which most of the action was played. A large number of candle lanterns hung at various heights and depths throughout the stage space, and remained lit for the entire show.

Tuesdays and Sundays

A sky of glowing lanterns. William and Mary are discovered sitting,
their eyes closed. Slowly, they awake.

William: Where are we?

Mary: Heaven?

William: Where are we?

Mary: Hell?

William: Where are we?

Both: …Earth.

William: Margate.

Mary: A rural community called

Both: Margate.

Mary: It's gorgeous. Beautiful winding roads

William: can't go straight

Mary: tranquil flowing rivers

William: field after field of potatoes

Mary: a rural community

William: like any other rural community—

Mary: —none like this one

William: …peaceful

Mary: …Heaven.

Beat.

Mary: a Tuesday

William: …yes, a Tuesday

Mary: that's where

William: New Year's Eve

Mary: going to the Bryenton's

William: yes

Mary: New Year's Eve

William: going to the Bryenton's

Mary: yes

Both: A TUESDAY!

William: Farm boys scrub the rich red dirt from their bodies

Mary: daughters of the farmers don their very best frocks

William: slick down their hair

Mary: fresh-faced

William: bundle up

Mary: for the cold

William: say goodnight to their parents with a promise to behave

Mary: and leave in time to arrive before the sun goes down…

William: my friend Francis at the gate, with a bottle of rum

Mary: with my older brother Jacob, we walk up Mud Road

William: sipping on the way

Mary: nervous and giddy

Both: the sun setting

William: and the moon, Francis, look!

Both: the sun and the moon!

Mary: we walk by the light of the sun and the moon…

Both: A NEW YEAR'S EVE DANCE AT MR. AND MRS. BRYENTON'S!

William: admission 25 cents

Mary: parents and grandparents, widows and pets

William: admission 25 cents?

Mary: bachelors and maids and infants and lovers

Both: EVERYONE WELCOME

Mary: Fiddling, punch, piano, a family affair

William: little girls dance on their fathers' feet

Mary: little boys run from their mothers' grasp

William: the older girls, whispers in the corner

Mary: the older boys, stealing drinks out back

Both: We meet

William: with a glance

Mary: by chance

William: by the punch

Both: We meet

Beat.

William: You're a Tuplin, right?

Mary: That's right, how'd you know?

William: I saw you come in with your brother.

Mary: You know my brother?

William: Yes.

Beat.

Mary: he gets me some punch

William: I get her some punch

Mary: he spills on my hand

William: I do?

Mary: Yes you do but don't notice so neither do I

Both: We stand there

Beat.

Mary: I've seen you before, what's your name?

William: Of course, how do you do, I'm—William Millman.

Mary: Mary Tuplin.

William: Pleased to make your acquaintance.

Mary: "William meet Mary. Mary meet William."

William: Thank you, Mr. Bryenton, we just met, sir, thank you. "She's soon to be seventeen, William, she's growing up quick!"

Mary: Thank you, Mrs. Bryenton, he knows we just met.

Both: "Well, well, carry on. This party's a success!"

William: "my dear"

Mary: "mutter mutter"

William: "my dear"

Mary: "mutter mutter"

Both: Alone

Beat.

Mary: William Millman.

William: Mary Tuplin. —feet beneath the table

Mary: soft words in the corner

William: I make her laugh

Mary: look at those couples, dancing so close

William: I give her a drink

Mary: a smile

William: a hand through the hair

Mary: getting to know you, sweet, exciting, soft, intriguing, getting to know

William: trying to get

Mary: getting to know

William: trying to get

Both: Flirting.

William: Francis, my friend, just stands in the doorway

Mary: Francis, his friend

Both: just stands in the doorway

William: and stares at the girl playing fiddle

Mary: my older brother Jacob

Both: finds a girl of his own

William: Jacob, her brother

Both: is not a good chaperone! …

Mary: Just before midnight!

William: all of us standing

Mary: music stopped, lights low

William: Mrs. Bryenton standing on a chair

Mary: Mr. Bryenton beside, holding up his watch

William: just before midnight!

Both: Ten…nine…eight…

Mary: William takes my hand in his

Both: seven…six…five

Mary: I look at him, looking at me, we smile, we count

Both: four…three…two

Mary: no one's looking

Both: one

Mary: he kisses me

William: Happy New Year…

Beat.

Mary: HE KISSES ME…

William: Happy New Year.

Beat.

Mary: We dance!

William: she dances, I try

Mary: we dance, till forever, we dance till forever and a day with my head on his shoulder, his hands on my back till forever

William: till four

Mary: till forever and

Both: our eyes closed

Mary: we kiss, till forever, my tiptoes, his hands, we kiss till forever and a day till forever

William: till four…and then I walk her home!

Mary: he walks me home! I am sixteen going on seventeen.

William: I am eighteen going on nineteen.

Mary: he's handsome

William: she's…giddy!

Mary: he's…handsome!

William: she's…!

Mary: William Millman.

William: Mary Tuplin.

Mary: You're walking me home.

William: So I am.

Mary: How many girls have you walked home in all your eighteen going on nineteen years?

William: I've walked home my share of girls.

Mary: Have you really?

William: No.

Beat.

Both: A WALK HOME AT FOUR IN THE MORNING

William: snow beneath our boots

Mary: my arm within his

William: our breath in the air

Mary: the moon guiding us along Mud Road

William: Did you see, earlier?

Mary: On the walk here?

Medina Hahn as Mary and Daniel Arnold as William in *Tuesdays and Sundays*, NeXtFest 2000 (Photograph courtesy of Wojtek Kozlinski)

William: The sunset?

Mary: And the moon? I saw!

William: Me too!

Mary: I saw!

William: "Yes, I saw t-t-too!"

Mary: yells Francis from behind, following behind

William: I can't believe I hang out with him!

Mary: Francis hears him and hollers

William: "I heard th-that!"—Go home!

Mary: William yells and I tell him—Be nice.

William: He told my folks he'd look after me so that's what he's doing.

Mary: Need looking after, do you?

William: According to my folks—Go home!

Mary: he yells again with the bark of a man not a child not a youth but a man

William: Just go.

Mary: Francis yells back

William: "Mama's b-b-boy!"

Beat.

William: on the bridge to cross the river…

Both: that bridge

Mary: to cross the river…

William: we kick snow from the deck…

Both: watch it fall to the water below

Mary: and keep on

William: before Francis catches up…

Mary: we talk

William: and we tease

Mary: about respectability and properness

William: at four in the morning with rum punch on our breath…we talk seriously a while

Mary: about the meaning of life

William: So who are you, Mary?

Mary: Just a girl, I think.

William: Don't think too much or you won't be…just a girl…

Beat.

Mary: he confuses me

William: …we don't talk at all

Beat.

Mary: he talks of his passion

William: I play piano at service!

Mary: Oh, that's where I've seen you!

William: Mr. Bryenton teaches me, and I'm getting quite good! I don't play every Sunday but pretty soon I will.

Mary: Yes, I knew I'd seen you before, yes, you play quite well. I remember, you play quite well indeed.

William: Thank you, Mary Tuplin.

Mary: You're welcome, William Millman.

William: I find this quite funny so I laugh and she—

Mary: You're laugh is funny.

William: —she makes fun of my laugh

Mary: Your laugh is funny.

William: Come now, Mary, don't tease.

Mary: I'm not teasing, William, I'm telling the truth.

William: The truth? And you call yourself a respectable girl.

Mary: I am.

William: Don't you know the "respectable" never tell the truth?

Mary: Yes they do.

William: No, it's what makes them respectable, "Never tell the truth."

Mary: You know nothing.

William: My my, we've grown up on different sides of the river that's for sure.

Mary: That's for sure indeed. You talk nonsense.

William: I may be a little drunk.

Mary: …and I give him a smile

William: and I try to wink but it's four in the morning and I'm quite tired so both eyes go

Both: blink

William: instead of a wink

Both: …and we smile…

Mary: …simply walk in silence now, down Mud Road, arm in arm

William: past the Black Horse Inn

Mary: all of its lights out

William: How is it that we've never met before?

Mary: I'm nearly three years younger than you.

William: That's no reason, I've known girls way younger than you…

Mary: I've no wish to know what you mean by that.

Beat.

William: This your gate?

Mary: Yes it is. —we walk up the lane

William: I tell Francis to wait, he sits down at the gate and pulls out a pipe, "good l-l-luck" he says and I tell him— shut up

Mary: we walk up the lane

William: right up to the door

Mary: out of Francis' sight

Both: we stand there

Beat.

William: she seems a bit nervous

Mary: does he want to come in?

William: I smile at her, I can't help it

Mary: he laughs

William: I smile

Mary: that funny laugh

William: I smile

Mary: and I laugh too and I open the door

William: she opens the door

Mary: Do you want to come in?

William: yes, yes I do very much.

Mary: he says nothing

William: yes, yes I do very much.

Mary: he says nothing—Well don't just stand there letting in the cold air.

William: I enter her house

Mary: he enters my house!

William: I enter her house!

Mary: my parents asleep, I close the door

William: she closes the door, pitch black

Mary: I light the lamp

Beat.

William: Nice place.

Mary: Thank you. Fire's out, but it's warmer than out there anyway. Do you want to take your boots off?

William: yes, yes I do very much.

Mary: William, your boots, do you want to take them off?

William: I'd like to Mary, thanks…but I shouldn't stay for long, I don't want Francis to freeze to death.

Mary: All right.

William: And my folks will be worried as well. I should be getting home. It must be past four o'clock.

Mary: All right, all right. I just thought you might like to warm up your feet.

William: They're fine. Thank you.

Mary: How long have you to walk?

William: Well, we're up past Warren's Mill, so from here it's probably a good hour and a bit.

Mary: Oh dear, I'm sorry, you needn't have taken me.

William: No, it was no trouble, I rather liked it…. You're some pretty, Mary Tuplin.

Mary: Please, you mustn't compliment me.

William: Why not?

Mary: One shouldn't be paid a compliment if one is undeserving.

William: And you're undeserving…? You're not. You're beautiful, Mary. You are.

Mary: Can we talk about something else?

William: Like what?

Mary: I don't know, anything.

William: Actually I should get going.

Mary: You just got in. You can't be warm yet.

William: No, I really should. My mother won't go to bed till I'm home.

Mary: Really?

William: Yes.

Mary: How awful. My parents usually retire before any of us.

William: Hm.

Mary: They're very sound sleepers as well…nothing can wake them…

William: Not my parents…. All right, I must be off.

Mary: his hand on my cheek, it's cold but it's nice

William: I step closer to her, her breath on my face

Mary: and he leans towards, looking at me

William: my eyes open

Mary: looking at me, I can't breathe

William: her breath on my face

Mary: I can't breathe

William: her breath in the

Both: air

Mary: I can't breathe

Beat.

William: I leave

Mary: we talk first

Beat.

William: then I leave

Mary: we talk, "a sleigh ride on Sunday," he says, "I'll come pick you up. This Sunday evening I'll come by with a sleigh and we'll go for a ride," and I agree and I agree and I agree!

William: she seems not to mind that she'll see me again! … "Sunday evening with a sleigh then," I say, "Sunday evening…"

Mary: Yes.

Beat.

William: a walk home in the cold, I puff from the pipe

Mary: I creep up the stairs, listen at the door

William: teasing from Francis, "short v-v-visit, s-s-sent home," those sorts of things

Mary: my parents snoring, I open the door and crawl into bed

William: but she wanted me back

Mary: and I lie awake to the sound of my parents asleep in the bed next to mine and I think

William: on Sunday I say she wishes to see me again and so there

Mary: is this love?

William: and I'm lying awake, I can't get to sleep

Mary: William Millman

William: Mary Tuplin

Both: I can't get to sleep. Is this love?

Beat.

William: A GENTLEMAN CALLER ON A SUNDAY EVENING!

Mary: A GENTLEMAN CALLER ON A SUNDAY EVENING!

William: without a sleigh

Mary: he never brought a sleigh!

William: I came though, I came, late Sunday, the family

Mary: he never brought a sleigh

William: I'm sorry

Mary: so we sit at home with my family and talk, John Junior running around, Jacob still peeling potatoes for being a bad chaperone, my parents fussing, my older sister Christy making eyes, my God

William: I'm sorry, I came though didn't I?

Mary: yes, he came!

Both: A GENTLEMAN CALLER ON A SUNDAY EVENING!

Mary: Goodnight Papa. Well that was exciting.

William: It was.

Mary: I'm so sorry, I do apologize. My family is not used to seeing boys around the house.

William: No bother.

Mary: Nerve racking.

William: Are you cold?

Mary: Mm. Father puts the fire out well before he goes to bed. Can't imagine why? Says it saves firewood. Stingy old man. I'm sorry it's so cold.

William: I'm fine. Probably does it to force you to retire early, don't you think?

Mary: Well it's not going to work tonight.

William: …I can stay for a while, if that's what you're getting at. My folks think I'm with John Profit tonight.

Mary: John Profit?

William: Yes, a friend of mine.

Mary: He is my teacher!

William: Oh yes, I guess he would be now, just started teaching.

Mary: Yes, just this year. He's handsome, William, he's a friend of yours?

William: we talk about John and my friends and the folks we both know

Mary: How is it possible that we've never met before?

William: …I'm going to not be respectable here and tell you the truth.

Mary: All right.

William: I tell her the truth.

Mary: All right.

William: I tell her I've seen her, I've seen her before.

Mary: I know.

William: No, I've seen her before. I'd stare. Quite a lot.

Mary: Cut it out, you did not.

William: I did too, I tell her…and when I saw her walk into the Bryenton's that evening, that Tuesday evening, that New Year's Eve, I thought: this is my chance, I thought: I must speak to her, I may never get to again.

Mary: Do stop it. Did you really?

William: Yes! I thought: I may never get this chance again, and that's when I gathered enough courage to appoach her.

Mary: Plus you were quite drunk.

William: A little perhaps. Courage, you know—but I tell her the truth, a little embarrassing but it is the truth.

Mary: My father doesn't approve of drinking.

William: Well I'm not courting your father, am I?

Mary: Oh so you're *courting* me, are you, well it's my mother who wouldn't approve of that…. They liked you though, I think, mother and father.

William: Your father hardly said a word to me.

Mary: That's a good sign though. And when I told Christy about you she immediately spread it like wildfire to the rest of my brothers and sisters that you were my "boyfriend," so that's why they've been looking at you and giggling all night. I'm sorry.

William: That's fine, I rather enjoyed it. I love John Junior! he's so sweet, how old is he?

Mary: Just turned three.

William: They're wild at that age, eh?

Mary: Oh, he was tame tonight. You should see him when he eats a candy or two, he's uncontrollable.

William: I love him!

Mary: Yes, definitely the wild one of us all. Well, the others were a little giddy tonight too, you understand—Why didn't you bring your sleigh?! You promised!

William: I never promised.

Mary: I know, it's all right, maybe next time.

William: Oh, so there will be a next time, will there?

Mary: I never said that. I said maybe. If you're good.

William: Ah.

Mary: Meaning you've still got a chance to redeem yourself tonight.

William: …All right.

Beat.

William: So the family seems to not mind me, eh?

Mary: It appears that way, can't imagine why…

William: …I like the way you smile.

Mary: You're always complimenting me, you must stop it.

William: Why?

Mary: …I like it.

Beat.

William: It is getting quite chilly in here actually.

Mary: It might be warmer in the parlour. The fire's probably still kind of warm and there's blankets if you'd like…

William: …Sounds lovely.

They touch.

William: keep your eyes on the girl

Mary: this look in his eyes

William: grab onto her hand

Mary: and my hand reaching out

William: letting go, reaching out

Mary: and we sink

William: round the front, to her stomach, her neck

Mary: away slowly down

William: slip her under

Mary: we're gone

William: in my arms, in the air

Mary: and we sink

William: round the front, to her stomach, her neck

Mary: away slowly down

William: slip her under

Mary: we're gone, and we sink

William: round the front, to her stomach, her neck

Mary: and we sink

William: round the front, to her stomach

Mary: we're gone, and we sink

William: slowly down, to her stomach, we're gone

Mary: and we sink slowly down

William: slip her under

Mary: we're gone, for eternity

William: gone

Mary: till forever

William: till

Beat.

William: "Mary?"

Mary: my father calls down in the middle of the night

William: "Mary, it's past midnight, why aren't you in bed?"

Mary: Oh God, get going!—we scramble and pray he won't come down the stairs

William: trip over my trousers—Where are my boots?

Mary: Get them on outside, quickly now, quickly!

William: I thought you said nothing could wake them— "Mary!?"

Mary: I *lied* get outside, quickly, outside.

William: she lied?

Mary: just a fib—Coming, Pa!

William: the rush of cold air, my feet in the snow, hurry round the back to the shadow of a tree and I stop. Breathe.

Mary: listen for movement upstairs…there is none— Coming!…so carefully now fold the blankets…tiptoe upstairs to the bedroom I share with my parents, and explain…

William: no noise in the house, must've gone back to sleep…throw my coat on the ground, wrestle my boots onto my soaking feet, do up my shirt, shake my coat off, put it on, and make my way home…

Mary: Sorry to frighten you, Papa. We were talking downstairs, we lost track of time.

Beat.

William: and on Tuesday…that Tuesday I walk down Mud Road towards Mary's

Mary: Sorry to frighten you, Papa, we lost track of time.

William: and I stop at the bridge, that same bridge we kicked snow from…at the end of the bridge, and look back

Mary: is this love?

William: and I carve it on the wood, under the deck, on Tuesday…that Tuesday I go out and I carve it under the bridge with my knife

Mary: is this love?

William: Mary Tuplin

Mary: William Millman

William: January 5th, 1887

Mary: on Tuesday

William: I carve it

Both: that Tuesday

Mary: I tell my sister Christy

William: on Tuesday

Mary: I'm in love!

William: I lie down and reach up and I carve it—Mary Tuplin!

Mary: William Millman!

William: January 5th, 1887—and as soon as I carve it…I know it is true

Mary: it is true! …it is true, I'm in love!

Beat.

Mary: Francis, where's William? Why hasn't he come by?

William: next Sunday the Bryentons take me aside

Mary: I saw him at church and he turned the other way.

William: they ask how things are with the young Tuplin girl— Oh, I visited her, met her family and all.

Mary: My family liked him, they wonder where he is.

William: I cared for her family, though her father quite scared me.

Mary: He needn't be scared of my father, he's fine.

William: And I quite cared for Mary

Mary: Does he not care for me?

William: Yes, I cared quite a lot…but she did not feel the same towards me… "Oh poor boy, that's too bad…but more time for your practice," Mr. Bryenton chuckles and I chuckle too and sit down to the piano and play…

Mary: If he feels like it, Francis, tell him he's welcome…tell him he can write.

William: not wanting to write, too scared to visit, I go to John Profit

Mary: John Profit

William: my friend

Mary: my teacher

Both: John Profit

William: Tell Mary Tuplin I feel it was a mistake.

Mary: whispers "William Millman feels it was a mistake."

William: I can't see her anymore

Mary: "He can't see you anymore."

William: I don't like her.

Mary: …"doesn't like you."

Beat.

William: Francis brags, "I've become p-p-pretty good friends with that mmMary Tuplin."

Mary: Christy, what does this mean?

William: "She j-j-jokes about you with her sssisters and ffffriends, William."

Mary: Oh my God, are you sure, Christy? oh my God.

William: "She g-g-giggles about you behind the—church on Sundays, yes I've become *quite close* friends with Mary."

Mary: Oh my God, Christy, please don't tell, please don't tell, are you sure?

William: but I try to forget about her

Mary: William? please, William?

William: and I try to not think about her

Mary: Francis, where's William?

William: and I try to not dream about her

Mary: Mr. Profit, where's William?

William: I am trying to forget about her!

Mary: Mr. Bryenton, it is imperative that I speak with William Millman!

William: "William, it is 'imperative' that Mary Tuplin speak with you!"

Mary: but I don't tell the reason

William: "She would not tell the reason."

Both: Please

William: I am trying to forget about her.

Mary: "He is trying to forget about you, Mary. It seems you may have broken his heart. My advice would be to send him a letter, mutter mutter, a letter."

William: don't send me a letter

Mary: William, Dear William

William: don't send me a letter

Mary: William, Dear William

William: I don't even read it. I lean out my window and by the light of the moon, strike a match and the flame…

Mary: Dear William

William: I don't even read it

Beat.

William: I help out my father on the farm

Mary: tansy, quinine, pennyroyal, rue…ergot of rye, cotton root, savin

William: take care of my mother—"William, I'm fine, now go learn your theory."

Mary: some field, or swamp, or grove contains the needful poison; and forthwith it is swallowed.

William: and I practice piano

Mary: if medicines fail: bleedings, hot baths, violent exercises, consumption of large quantities of gin

William: save money for college

Mary: if these don't prevail: attempt a dilation of the cervix with slippery elm, a sponge tent, or catheter

William: and time just goes by

Mary: if still not beyond the sixteenth week

William: and time just goes by

Mary: "Too much time has gone by," Christy says… "It's too late now to try anything else."

Beat.

Mary: I'm sorry, Mama, I'm sorry, I'm sorry—Papa!

William: "Mary Tuplin's dropped from school," says John Profit

Mary: I tried to be rid of it, Christy and I we tried.

William: Is she sick? I ask John. He's not sure

Mary: William Millman, you remember…he came about New Year's.

William: he asks, "What happened at New Year's?"

Both: and I breathe…we were downstairs in the parlour, under some blankets

William: "You're teasing!" he says—No I'm not.

Both: We did, it's the truth.

Mary: I'm sorry.

William: "Your parents will kill you if they ever find out!"

Both: I know

Mary: "You'll take care of it, Mary, or you know I will."

Both: I know

Mary: father

Both: I know…

Mary: and a letter to the Bryentons—Tell William to meet me

Both: on Sunday

William: Mr. Bryenton takes me aside

Mary: Tell him to meet me down at my gate.

William: "You must meet Mary Tuplin down at her gate!"

Both: Why?

Mary: Tell him why!

William: And she's saying it's mine?!

Mary: It's William Millman's for sure.

Beat.

William: a gentleman caller on a Sunday evening

Mary: waiting for William

William: I walk down Mud Road

Mary: six months since that night

William: six months, half a year since I walked down this road, we kicked snow from this bridge, I crept under this bridge with my knife

Mary: six months

William: half a year

Both: and you find it goes by with the blink of an eye...

William: I spoke not one word to Mary in that whole half a year

Mary: not one word...

William: a gentleman caller on a Sunday evening

Mary: a gentleman caller on a Sunday evening...

William: Thank you for meeting.

Mary: Thank you for coming.... How are you?

William: Fine. You?

Mary: I've been better. Keeping busy?

William: Yes. On the piano a lot more these days. Three times a week. Hoping to be accepted to college this autumn.... You're feeling all right?

Mary: Under the circumstances.

William: How's your family?

Mary: Little John is sick, you remember him?

William: John Junior? Of course I do. Is he bad?

Mary: Yes, very bad.

William: Oh no, I'm sorry. Give him my love, and my regards to the family as well.

Mary: How's *your* family?

William: Doing all right…. Yes, they're doing all right…. You look healthy.

Mary: Do I?

William: Yes.

Mary: Thank you. I don't feel it.

Beat.

William: and it's questions upon questions upon talk about *blame*

Mary: William—

William: No, that's what Mr. Bryenton said is all, that the blame is on me…. It's funny. The Bryentons think it's partly *their* fault: they still believe *they* introduced us.

Mary: and it's answers upon questions upon talk about *truth*

William: And you're saying it's mine?

Mary: Yes, that's the truth.

William: Truth?

Mary: Yes.

William: Not just teasing?

Mary: No.

William: You're sure?

Mary: Yes.

William: And does anyone know…that you're saying it was me?

Mary: The Bryentons know, and my family of course.

William: You told your family you thought it was me?

Mary: Yes.

William: I look up to the house, her father in the window

Mary: I turn around, Papa staring at us—And do *your* parents know?

William: They can't know, they'd kill me. That's why I couldn't see you again.

Mary: Why?

William: My folks…

Mary: Yes.

William: They want me to go to college. They say a social life gets in the way.

Mary: Truth?

William: Yes.

Mary: The only reason you couldn't see me again? Your folks?

William: Yes.

Mary: Truth?

William: Yes…not only that. I felt bad.

Mary: Bad?

William: It was a sin, Mary.

Mary: …It doesn't have to be.

Beat.

William: and her hand on her tummy

Mary: It's six months for sure.

William: the wind rushes by

Mary: with this look in his eyes

William: I thought I was quite careful

Mary: this look in his eyes

William: I thought I was quite careful.

Mary: Sorry?

William: I said I thought I was quite careful, Mary. I mean, I tried to do just what they all say, to…pull myself out before like…

Mary: Well—

William: No, I was quite careful, Mary. I made sure.

Mary: William…you're the only one I've been with that way.

William: …I don't know, Mary.

Mary: About what?

William: Like I said, I was quite careful.

Mary: William.

William: No, Mary—

Mary: William, you realize what you are saying about me.

Beat.

William: How is Francis?

Mary: Sorry?

William: From what I hear you and Francis were pretty sweet on each other.

Mary: What are you talking about?

William: He tells me you became quite close friends.

Mary: I haven't seen him for months.

William: Why not?

Mary: I don't know, he stopped calling round. WHAT did he tell you?

William: He told me you had become *quite close.*

Mary: Oh my God.

William: I'm only telling you what he said.

Mary: Well, he's LYING, William. This child is yours.

William: …All right Mary, I've got to meet you some other time. My folks will be wondering where I am.

Mary: William. My father wanted me to make sure you knew some things.

William: All right, what?

Mary: That this will cost money.

William: I know.

Mary: And that he and my mother will not take on too much of the responsibility.

William: All right.

Mary: And that...*my* reputation will not suffer because of this.

William: All right.

Mary: So they wonder how you feel about me. And how I feel about you. Us. They wonder if it's a possibility. I told them it wasn't really, after all, you didn't want to see me again, but—

William: No, I did want to, Mary...I couldn't. Listen, I really have to be off. I'll meet you on Tuesday, is that all right? I'm away tomorrow, doing my conservatory, but I can meet you Tuesday evening, all right?

Mary: Sure.

William: Sundown?

Mary: Sure. Meet me here.

William: All right. See you then.

Mary: turn back up the lane. Papa still stands there

William: head back up Mud Road, quicken my pace

Mary: Papa still stands there—William? What do I tell my father?

William: We're going to meet on Tuesday and work something out.

Mary: —we're going to meet on Tuesday and work something out

William: Hey...I hope John Junior feels better.

Mary: Me too. Thank you.

Both: We're going to meet on Tuesday and work something out.

Beat.

Mary: and on Tuesday

William: at sunset

Both: that Tuesday

William: I make my way towards Mary's, down Mud Road, across that bridge

Mary: wait by the gate, I'm alone at home, caring for the Bryenton's little one…seems they feel the sudden desire to train me in mothering

William: the breeze is nice, fans the sweat from my face

Mary: just before sunset

William: and there she stands

Mary: by the gate

William: with a little one in her arms

Mary: She's the Bryentons', I'm taking care of her.

William: that's what she'll look like, carrying a child

Mary: I can see it in his eyes

William: beautiful…and she blushes, she almost blushes but

Mary: My family will be home any minute.

William: So?

Mary: You don't want to be here, trust me.

William: What's wrong?

Mary: Go hide in the bushes and I'll meet you there.

William: and the moment she says it, she turns back to the house, so I run across the road to the trees, duck down

Both: and I wait

Mary: at the window for my folks to arrive—Down to the river!

William: she whispers

Mary: I do?

William: yes, you do

Mary: Down to the river!

William: Why? What's the hurry?

Mary: My father just arrived, he wants to talk with you in person, he'll be out any minute.

William: and I quicken my pace

Mary: move a branch from my way

William: it snaps back in my face

Mary: we duck under leaves, over roots, through the trees

William: Why does he want to talk with me?

Mary: He doesn't think we can work something out by ourselves. He wants to get your parents involved.

William: Whoa.

Mary: I know and I tried to tell him that we'd work it out, just you and me.

Both: take a quick look back

William: Does he know where you are?

Mary: I ran out without saying a word. Come, this way.

William: …and we come to the clearing, to the bank of the river

Mary: and we stand by the trees, and the river runs by

William: across the river, a field

Mary: across the field, more trees

William: and above the trees

Both: the sun caresses the skyline…

William: So he's pretty serious, eh?

Mary: Well, I think he's got a right to be, William.

William: "Mary?"

Mary: my father calls from the road

William: "Mary, where are you?"

Beat.

"You come back to the house this instant, Mary."

Beat.

"William Millman."

Beat.

"I know you're out there."

Mary: William.

William: "I know that you're out there."

Mary: William. Listen to me. He won't come down here, and even if he did, we'd hear him through the trees. So calm down, sit beside me and let's talk or we'll never get back up there.

William: and she smiles

Mary: and he laughs

William: I…smile

Mary: that funny laugh

Beat.

William: Francis.

Mary: Francis? What about him?

William: We had a good talk.

Mary: You still believe— ?

William: No. I don't know what to believe.

Mary: No?

William: No, I don't know who or what to believe.

Mary: and it's talk of the letter

William: Did you send me a letter?

Mary: A letter?

William: Around March, I think?

Mary: Yes.

William: It wasn't from Francis?

Mary: No.

William: Truth?

Mary: Yes. You thought it was Francis?

William: No, I didn't know. I didn't even read it.

Mary: What?

William: I didn't even read it. I burned it.

Mary: You didn't even read it?

William: No.

Mary: So you never knew?

William: What.

Mary: That you were to meet me at the Bryenton's cream social.

William: No.

Mary: That I was expecting a child, you never even knew?

William: Not till Mr. Bryenton told me on Sunday.

Mary: Truth?

William: Yes.

Mary: And why did you burn it?

William: I was trying to forget about you. I thought it might bring me some peace.

Mary: Some peace?

William: I had a suspicion it was from Francis anyway.

Mary: My letter? From Francis?

William: Yes, it could have been Francis taking one of his pokes at me.

Mary: How?

William: He'd always rub it in that he was calling on you and that you and he would laugh about me.

Mary: Laugh?

William: Yes, he told me you'd poke fun at the time we spent together.

Mary: Poke fun?

William: You'd giggle behind the church with your sisters and friends.

Mary: No, William, no. No, not at all. I cared for you. My family cared for you.

Beat.

William: That man up there actually cared for me?

Mary: Believe it or not…

William: I cared for you too, Mary. —and the breeze through her hair

Mary: my reflection in his eyes

William: I have to look away

Mary: needing a touch

William: wanting to reach

Mary: trying to stay

William: May I?

She nods. He reaches out. She looks down to her tummy.

Mary: And here I thought you meant…by not meeting me, by not seeing me…I thought you meant I should get rid of it.

William: No. I didn't even know. I had no idea…. Why didn't you?

Mary: What do you mean?

William: Get rid of it…

Mary: It wasn't for lack of trying…

Beat.

William: noise by the road

Mary: up near the road, voices of men, walking through trees

William: They're coming down here!

Mary: My father with others, he must really be angry.

William: Oh God, let's go, let's go Mary now!

Mary: Where?

William: Away, down the river, along the bank to the bridge.

Mary: My father will kill me, we should really head back.

William: What?! and say what?

Mary: We're sorry, we've worked something out, he'll understand.

William: You mean *lie*?

Mary: No, we've worked something out, we care for each other. Come on, he's going to kill me for running away.

William: Kill you? he'll kill me!

Mary: Don't worry, William, you tell him what you just told me, he'll be fine, we'll be together.

William: …Mary, follow me.

Mary: Where?

William: Away, just follow, we need to talk more.

Mary: What is wrong?

William: Your father and his hunting party that's what's wrong!

Mary: No, William. What is wrong?

William: I can't do this, I can't!

Mary: What are you talking about?

William: I can't be with you, Mary. I can't and I won't.

Mary: …this look in his eyes, he's telling the truth, not very respectable but he's telling the truth

William: I can't, I'm sorry. Look, either follow me now and we'll work something out, or we'll talk later, I can't be standing here like a dope when your father comes crashing out of those trees.

Mary: and his frightened young face

William: her confused little eyes—Mary, I'm sorry just let me explain.

Mary: and the snap of a branch, even closer now

William: I grab her hand, we run up the river

Mary: holding on tight, he pulls me along, I stumble on the rocks and cry out in pain

William: but I'm still holding on, we scramble up the bank, in the trees, out of sight

Mary: one hand in his, the other on my belly

William: we crouch in the trees…. Are you all right?

Mary: I'll be fine.

William: Are you sure?

Mary: I'll be fine.

William: her pain, her breathing, her eyes on the ground

Mary: I feel him staring at me

William: Follow me further and we'll work something out.

Mary: he moves the branches away from my face

William: and we creep in silence till we get to the bridge

Mary: no one around

William: we dash for the bank

Mary: slide under the deck

William: and up out of sight

Both: …we sit there, still, still holding hands…

Mary: the river below us

William: the bridge just above

Mary: and he nods to some carving on the underside of the wood

Both: …Mary Tuplin, William Millman—January 5th, 1887…

William: I carved it the Tuesday after…I was on my way to call on you, and I stopped here and carved it…

Beat.

William: I need to leave home, Mary. I need to leave Margate.

Mary: Why?

William: I'm going to college in autumn for my music and I'm not coming back.

Mary: I'll come with you.

William: You can't.

Mary: Why not?

William: My father runs a tight house, Mary, a tight, strict house.

Mary: So? So you're leaving.

William: That's right, I am. And I have money enough for myself and…no others.

Mary: My parents will give me some money if it means going with you, I'm sure they will.

William: Mary…No.

Mary: Then what do we do?

William: I can give you a little money.

Mary: I don't want your money.

William: That's all I can offer.

Mary: I'll wait till you're back.

William: I'm not coming back.

Mary: Why can't you stay here?

William: I've told you already.

Mary: Have you?

William: I'm going to college, I need to leave home.

Mary: And why can't I come? …William!

William: No!

Mary: Why can't I come?!…I have an unclaimed child in my belly, William. That's how my mother put it—unclaimed. Do you know what that means? It means I couldn't even go to the funeral today. I had to stay home. I couldn't even go to my own brother's funeral. My family is too embarrassed…

William: Funeral?

Mary: You never heard?

William: I've been away.

Mary: My little brother John died Sunday night.

William: Oh my God. And you couldn't go to his funeral?

Mary: I haven't been off the farm for a good while now. My parents have actually started to ignore me around the house.

William: Really?

Mary: You don't understand the shame, do you?

William: Yes I do, Mary.

Mary: But it's not written on your body.

William: …and the wind whistles lightly across the bridge picking up dust

Mary: carrying it along, across the river, the tiniest of ripples on the water

Both: and the sun sinks into the earth…

William: I want to run away with you. I want to just take you by the hand and walk up this river and never look back.

Mary: Then do it.

Beat.

William: footsteps on the road

Mary: pounding the earth, running above us, right on the deck

William: dirt trickles down from between the boards

Mary: sand in the light of the sun

William: voices of men

Mary: two, I think

William: one, Mr. Bryenton

Mary: the other my father…they mumble together

William: low voices and mutters

Both: they stop

William: ...Oh God

Both: silence

Mary: Dear God...

William: "William!"

Mary: "Mary!"

Both: they don't know we're here!

Mary: thank God

William: they keep on

Mary: cross the bridge

William: and keep on.... I think it's fair to say that I'm quite worried.

Mary: What are they doing?

William: I bet you ten to one, Mr. Bryenton is taking him to my house.

Mary: Really?

William: Yup.

Mary: I'm sorry.

William: Yup. That's not good.

Mary: What should we do?

William: I need to stop them. My folks can't know about this.

Mary: crawls out from under the deck

William: Listen, Mary, go home. I'll go catch up with them and say you're back. We're sorry we ran away and everything's settled.

Mary: Everything's not settled.

William: LIE, Mary, please. He'll understand if you're safe at home, it will be settled, he'll understand. Now go, Mary, go.

Mary: leaps onto the bridge, but I do not move

William: run a couple of steps

Daniel Arnold as William and Medina Hahn as Mary in *Tuesdays and Sundays*, NeXtFest 2000 (Photograph courtesy of Wojtek Kozlinski)

Mary: I do not move, he looks over his shoulder, he stops, I don't move

William: Mary, go. Please.

Mary: I don't move

William: Please Mary, go!

Mary: I don't move

William: Fine, I'll tell him you're here.

Mary: but before he can leave

William: she clutches her dress in her hand

Mary: I work my way up the bank

William: Careful, Mary, be careful.

Mary: up the bank to the road

William: she stands at the end of the bridge

Mary: he stands in the middle…and my hand reaching out

William: you let go, you reach out

Mary: letting go, reaching out

William: I don't move… and step back, I step back, going to run

Mary: I'm coming with you.

William: under her breath but I heard it

Mary: I'm coming with you.

William: No, Mary, you are going home. We'll work it out later.

Mary: one hand holding my dress, the other defiantly swinging at my side as I walk

William: Mary, calm down.

Mary: No, I'm coming with you, we're going to your house right now, let me by.

William: Mary.

Mary: No, we'll catch up with my father—let me go—we'll march right into your house—let go of me, William!

William: Mary, please, calm down, let's be reasonable—

Mary: ow!

William: Mary, stop it!

Mary: No! Go tell my father the truth, William!

William: You don't understand.

Mary: Go tell *your* father the truth!

William: You don't understand!

Mary: Then tell *me* the truth!

William: …I can't

Mary: and I cry out in pain

William: I can't

Mary: and he won't let me go

William: I can't

Mary: he won't

William: I can't

Mary: he will not let go

William: I can't

Mary: There's so many things you just can't do, why is that?

William: I don't know.

Mary: Fear?

William: Yes.

Mary: What have you got to be afraid of? —and this look in his eyes

William: …she won't let me go

Mary: William?

William: …she won't let me go

Mary: William?

William: …she sees

Mary: my God!

William: she runs

Mary: I run, down the bridge, to the road, along the bank

William: I follow, she's silent

Both: I'm screaming inside

Mary: I fly like the wind

William: I follow

Mary: I stumble on the rocks, then run on, don't look back

William: keep your eyes on the girl

Mary: don't look back

William: keep your eyes on the girl

Mary: a hand on my shoulder, I scream

William: I've got her, round the front, to her stomach, her neck

Mary: and we sink

William: round the front, to her stomach, her neck, to the water, the edge of the river and—

She screams.

William: I move but I'm not really there, ringing and gripping

Mary: I'm screaming inside

William: I can see my hands but they're so far away, under water, around her and under

Mary: I'm screaming inside

William: and it's loud, louder than anything, drowning out everything…and that's what you're doing, you breathe in the water

Mary: where am I?

William: you're there but your body

Mary: I'm gone

William: there's nothing

Mary: the water, the weight…the water takes everything

Beat.

William: and for a few breaths

Both: our child

Mary: has a few breaths

William: after your heart has stopped

Both: our child

William: for a few breaths

Mary: lives beyond its mother

Beat.

William: and I stand with her, I stand and I walk

Mary: with Mary with child in the blanket of your arms

William: I walk

Mary: till forever

William: for just a few steps

Mary: till forever

William: out into the water, and slip her under…your eyes

Mary: they're open, eyes open

William: your eyes

Mary: they're open, eyes open, looking up at you, wondering what you've done, being dragged slowly down…back on land you wander a bit

William: under the bridge

Mary: they'll find me, they will know, you will be blamed

William: should I have buried her?

Both: and it's not questions about life and death and love, it's not questions like that

Mary: that run through your mind, it's questions like

William: should I have buried her? she wouldn't be found if I'd buried her…

The lights fade slowly, till all that remains is a sky of glowing lanterns.

Biographies

BRADLEY MOSS is artistic director of Theatre Network and producer of NeXtFest, the Syncrude NeXt Generation Arts Festival.
Born in Montreal and raised in the Eastern Townships of Quebec,
he attended Bishop's University where he graduated with a BA in
DRAMA and BUSINESS HONOURS. Here he helped initiate and create ACTIV, a student drama festival focused on creating new work.
On two occasions, in 1996 and 1997, he returned to Bishop's as guest
artist and instructor. After graduation he first moved to Vancouver
where he acted in theatre and film and also founded the theatre
company Big Tree Productions, for which he directed *Provincetown
Playhouse, Texas Boy,* and *Waiting for Godot.* He came to Edmonton in
1992 to begin his MFA in DIRECTING at the University of Alberta,
with his thesis play, *The Queens,* produced at Studio Theatre in 1994.
The following year he directed *Stretch* with Andy Curtis and Neil
Grahn for the High Performance Rodeo in Calgary and joined
Theatre Network to begin work on the development of NeXtFest as
its first director and ongoing producer. During NeXtFest '98,
Bradley was appointed interim artistic director of Theatre Network
and artistic director in the spring of 1999. As an actor he performed
in Brad Fraser's *Martin Yesterday,* directed by the playwright at
Theatre Network in 1998, and later that year returned to Montreal
to play a leading role in the independent feature film *Gasp!,* written
and directed by Roy Cross. His first direction for Theatre Network
was *High Life* by Lee MacDougall, receiving six Sterling nominations
for the 1998-99 season, including Outstanding Production and
Outstanding Direction.

In the summer of 1999 he directed the hit Winnipeg and
Edmonton Fringe show *PileDriver!* by Wes Borg and Darrin Hagen,
nominated for Sterlings as Outstanding Fringe Production and
Outstanding Fringe Director. In the 1999-2000 season he directed
George F. Walker's *Problem Child* for a Theatre Network and
Workshop West co-production, and also for Theatre Network
Eugene Stickland's *A Guide To Mourning,* which received Sterling
nominations for Outstanding Production and Outstanding
Direction.

GLENDA STIRLING, originally from Lethbridge, Alberta, has spent most of the last nine years in Edmonton, with some time in Vancouver and London, England where her passion for physical theatre was born. She graduated from the University of Alberta in 1996 with a BA in DRAMA. Her first two opportunities to work in theatre came from Bradley Moss that same year: as a stage manager for NeXtFest '96 and as an actor in his production of *Tony 'n' Tina's Wedding* later that summer. She then went on to direct and produce *Smoke Damage* for her own company, Not This Not That. Working with Northern Light Theatre as corporate campaign and marketing manager for the next two seasons, she learned the skills of grant application, budgeting, and contracting artists. Glenda has directed or assistant directed over 20 theatre productions in the past five years, most often new work and physical theatre. These include, for NeXtFest, *No One Showed Up for the Anarchist Rally*, 1998, *Stale Mate*, 1999, and *The Dirt on Mo*, 2000, for Northern Light Theatre, *Ad Cabaret*, 1998, 1999 and *Urban Tales*, 1999, for Springboards Dance Festival, *Sssomething*, 1999, for One Yellow Rabbit Performance Theatre, *InKlezskavania*, 1999, for Keyano College, *Miracle on 34 Street* and for Walterdale Theatre, *Goodnight Desdemona (Good Morning Juliet)*, both in 2000.

She has also written three full-length plays: *Dark Isle*, The Globe Theatre/Curtain Razors, 1999; *Sticks, Stones, and Ancestor Bones*, Workshop West Theatre, SpringBoards, 2000; *The Longest One Night Stand in History*, NeXtFest New Play Cabaret, 2000; and two short works, *Here Be Dragons*, 1999, and *Fleece Boy*, 2000, Alberta Theatre Projects, Brief New Works. After spending two years as festival director for Theatre Network's Syncrude NeXt Generation Arts Festival, Glenda is now living in Calgary, where she is writing, directing, and producing plays, teaching movement, and assisting artistic director Ian Prinsloo at Theatre Calgary.

DANIEL ARNOLD is an Edmonton-based performer, playwright, and founding member of Dead English Theatre. He graduated from the University of Alberta with a BFA in ACTING from the University of Alberta in 2000. His other plays include *Not with a Bang, Not with a Whimper, but with a Dull Thud* and *Some Squishing Sounds*, for Edmonton Theatre Theatre, 1997; *War with Ricki and Rich*, a short film screened by the National Screen Institute; and "Bound," a one-man show in progress. *Tuesdays and Sundays* is his first collaboration with another writer and the first time he has worked with a dramaturge.

MEDINA HAHN is an Edmonton-based actor, dancer, and singer. She holds two performance degrees, a BFA in THEATRE from the University of Victoria and BFA in ACTING from the University of Alberta, where she first met classmate Daniel Arnold. While she has written in the past, *Tuesdays and Sundays* is her first completed and produced script. She hopes that the play will be one of many collaborations with Daniel Arnold and plans to continue her exploration of self-generated work.

SEAN CALLAGHAN graduated in 1998 from the University of Alberta with a BEd in ENGLISH. An Edmonton-born writer, he has spent much of the last two years in Japan, teaching English and writing. One of his first theatrical ventures was as producer and writer of *Peter Waal's Last Regret* in the 1993 Edmonton Fringe Festival. He has premièred two plays on the NeXtFest main stage: *"No. Please–"* in 1996 and *Opus 2. Karaoke Memories*, directed by Bill Kerr, in 1998, followed by a run at the Edmonton Fringe. His multimedia extravaganza, *Masquerade*, is scheduled to première at NeXtFest 2001. Currently he is working on an existential children's story while studying Japanese, phenomenology, and mathematics in a suburb of Tokyo.

CHRIS CRADDOCK is a playwright and performer who graduated with a BFA in ACTING from the University of Alberta in 1996. Following production of his plays *SuperEd*, 1996 and *Indulgences*, 1997, he set out to learn collaboration, writing with Darrin Hagen on *Tranny Get Your Gun* and with Wes Borg on *Ha!*, both for the 1998 Edmonton Fringe. He won a Sterling Award for his performance in *Ha!*, a one-man show about a prairie farm boy turned stand-up comic, performed also in Winnipeg, Calgary, Grande Prairie, and at the Edmonton Street Performers Festival. The 1999 Edmonton Fringe saw Craddock's directorial debut with *Men are Stoopid, Women are Cra-azy*, a funny examination of the gender wars co-written with Darrin Hagen, also presented at the Edmonton Comedy Arts Festival in 2000. He has written two full-length plays for Rapid Fire Theatre of Edmonton: *On Being a Peon*, a backstage comedy from the point of view of the walk-ons in a production of *Othello*, and his first play with songs, a satire entitled *The Critic*. The former was awarded a Sterling for Outstanding Production of a Collective in 1999, and the latter nominated for three Sterlings in 2000. Craddock also writes for teens. His plays for Azimuth Theatre of Edmonton, *The Day Billy Lived*, 1998, 1999, and *Wrecked*, 2000, have toured to schools all over western Canada. In collaboration with Wes Borg, he has been commissioned to write two plays for young audiences by Edmonton's Fringe Theatre Adventures: *The Monster Club I* and *II*, and he is continuing to adapt the novel *Summer of my Amazing Luck* by Miriam Toews, for Theatre Network. In the spring of 2000, Craddock was presented with the City of Edmonton Enbridge Award for Emerging Artist.

PAUL MATWYCHUK is originally from Hamilton, Ont., where he studied HONOURS HISTORY and ENGLISH at McMaster University. He moved to Edmonton to take CREATIVE WRITING at the University of Alberta under Greg Hollingshead, earning his MA in 1993. As an Edmonton actor and playwright he has written and performed one-man shows at five of the last six Edmonton Fringe Festivals: *The Muscular Stepmother*, 1995; *The Key to Violet's Apartment*, 1996; *Hit the Road to Dreamland*, 1997; *Euripedes Freakout*, 1999; and *Lingerie*, 2000. He earned Sterling nominations for Outstanding Fringe New Work and Outstanding Fringe Actor for *Eurpides Freakout* in 1999. He is currently managing editor of *Vue Weekly* where he writes about theatre, books and film.

ROSEMARY ROWE graduated with a BFA in DIRECTING from York University in 1997. She is the author of fourteen plays, the first of which, *Mrs. Dickerhoff Gets Up Close and Personal,* was the first teen-written play to be produced at Citadel Theatre's late Teen Festival of the Arts, 1992. Since then, she has written plays for Theatre Network's NeXtFest: *Benedetta Carlini: Lesbian Nun of Renaissance Italy!!!*, 1996; *Beaten With Pastry Under Cover of Darkness: A Tourist's Tale*, 1997; and *No One Showed Up for the Anarchist Rally*, 1998. She has written and directed plays for Edmonton's Dead English Theatre, of which she is a founding member: *Sir Walter Raleigh Tryeth Pretty Hard*, 1997; *Carlill v. the Carbolic Smokeball Company*, 1998; and *Tired of Rhetorical Questions?*, 2000. She has also written and directed seven plays for the Edmonton Fringe Festival, including *Selling Pyrogies to Gerard Depardieu*, 1994; *And Also, You're Evil*, 1996; and also for Fresh Fest, A Rose and Two Pansies of Toronto (where she now lives), the Montreal Fringe, and Infinitheatre of Montreal. Her most recent project is directing and dramaturging Paul Dunn's play *Boys* for Theatre Direct's 1999/2000 season in Toronto. Currently she is working on a new play, "Gush!"

Songwriter series: The Luann Kowalek Band. l to r are Chris Smith, Paul (Duke) Paetz, Luann Kowalek, Sherry Lee Heschel (Photograph courtesy of David Williamson)

The crowd at NeXtFest 2000, outside the Roxy Theatre (Photograph courtesy of David Williamson)